THE LOST TOMBS
OF THEBES
LIFE IN PARADISE

ZAHI HAWASS

Photographs by SANDRO VANNINI

THE LOST TOMBS OF THEBES
LIFE IN PARADISE

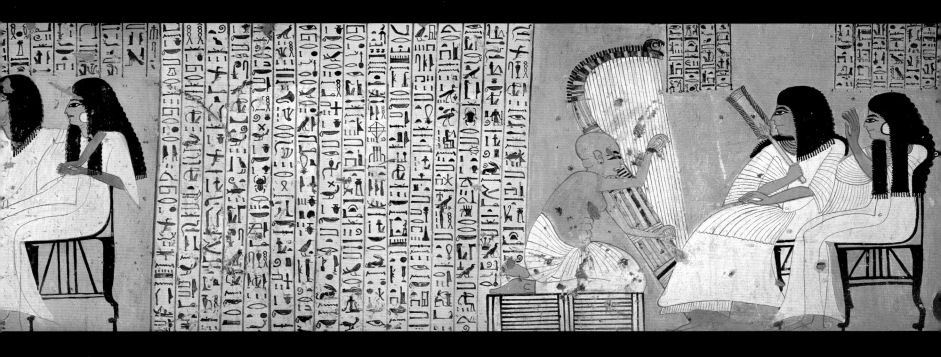

With 208 illustrations, 201 in color

Thames & Hudson

This book is dedicated to my friend Mark Linz

ACKNOWLEDGMENTS

I would like to thank the many people who helped me in the preparation of this book and who played an important role in its completion. First, I would like to thank the staff at Thames & Hudson. In addition, I am grateful to my staff in the scientific office of the Supreme Council of Antiquities, especially Dr. Tarek El Awady, Mohamed Megahed, Sherif Shaaben, Wesam Mehrez, and Heba Ahmed. I would also like to give very special thanks to my friend and colleague Janice Kamrin, who is working as my assistant in my office at the SCA, for editing my handwritten text.

ENDPAPERS
Detail of the painted ceiling from the tomb of Amenhotep Huy, Viceroy of Kush (TT 40).

PAGES 2–3
Detail of the painted ceiling from the tomb of Nefersekheru (TT 296).

TITLE PAGE: ABOVE
Detail of the decoration shown atop a shrine in a painting in the tomb of Irunefer (TT 290).

CENTER
A banqueting scene in the tomb of Inerkhau (TT 359).

BELOW
Detail of an orchard with various types of fruit trees, from the tomb of Sennedjem (TT 1).

RIGHT
The entrance to the tomb of Paser (TT 106), showing the tomb owner and his mother.

PAGES 8–9
Two fishermen haul in their catch with a net, from the tomb of Ipuy (TT 217).

First published in 2009 in hardcover in the United States of America by Thames & Hudson Inc., 500 Fifth Avenue, New York, New York 10110

thamesandhudsonusa.com

Library of Congress Catalog Card Number 2008911979

ISBN 978-0-500-05159-7

Printed and bound in China by C&C Offset Printing Co. Ltd.

CONTENTS

A detail of a scene from the tomb of Kheruef (TT 192),
Steward of the Great Royal Wife Tiye, showing the queen
holding the wrist of her husband, Amenhotep III.

INTRODUCTION
THE ETERNAL HOUSE OF THE SOUL

People are always eager to hear about the mysteries of the Valley of the Kings. News from the Valley, where Egypt's New Kingdom pharaohs were buried, is reported enthusiastically by the media and devoured avidly by the public. The spectacular discovery of the tomb of Tutankhamun in 1922 is, of course, to a large degree responsible for the fascination that this ancient necropolis holds for the general public. But many people do not know that the foothills of the Theban massif, just east of the royal tombs, are filled with unique and beautifully decorated tombs belonging to the people who served the pharaohs. Buried here are viziers, officials, courtiers, and even the workmen and artisans who carved and decorated the sepulchers of the kings. To date, approximately 900 tombs from many periods of Egyptian history have been unearthed in these rocky hills, and many more surely remain hidden.

The focus in this book is on around 80 of the more than 400 tombs that were tunneled into the cliffs for the elite of New Kingdom Egypt, when the pharaohs ruled the East. This Golden Age spanned the centuries from approximately 1550 to 1100 BC and comprised dynasties 18 through 20. While some of the Theban private tombs are well known, and contain familiar scenes, others have been lost almost completely to the eyes of the world. Many, while accessible, are closed to the public and are visited only sporadically by scholars. Others have been hidden under villages built above them over the past centuries. Of these modern villages, the most famous is el-Qurna, just west of the Ramesseum, where local people began to construct houses soon after foreign adventurers came to the Luxor area in their quest to rediscover the royal and private tombs. A number of the more notorious inhabitants of el-Qurna were well-known antiquities dealers and tomb robbers, since one of the reasons that houses were built on top of the tombs was so that they could be raided in secret. The most famous family of tomb robbers, the Abdel Rassouls, lived in this area, and later in this book I will tell you about my relationship with Sheikh Ali, one of its last surviving members.

The location of villages directly above the tombs has created many problems. For example, a two-story house was built over the beautifully decorated tomb of Amenhotep Huy, Viceroy of Kush under Tutankhamun; water from this house has done a great deal of damage to the decoration of the tomb chapel. Another person had dug a tunnel from his house to a nearby private tomb so that he could use it to store stolen antiquities. Others used the tombs beneath their houses as animal pens. In 2006, Ali el-Asfar, director of antiquities for the West Bank, informed me that a man from the village of el-Khokha had transformed his house, built directly above an unknown tomb, into a hotel. I was amazed that this could still happen, and had the matter taken to the police. There are many other stories regarding the history of these villages, some of which I will tell you in the last chapters of this book.

In 2008, the governorate of Luxor finished the construction of a new, modern village, located at el-Tarif, to the north of the Valley of the Kings. The majority of the costs for this village were paid for by the Supreme Council of Antiquities (SCA), the organization of which I am head, in order to save the tombs. The governor of Luxor moved the villagers of el-Qurna to new homes there and tore down the old houses – all but 25, which were left as testimony to the unique history of this area. A woman named Caroline Simpson has restored two of these houses and transformed them into a museum to keep the history of el-Qurna alive. It should come as no surprise to learn that when the old houses were removed, teams from the Supreme Council of Antiquities discovered beneath them a number of new tombs! I will tell you more of this story in Chapter 9.

The elite tombs of Thebes were tunneled into the rocky hillsides that rise above the floodplain on the West Bank of the Nile at modern Luxor. The rock in this area is mostly limestone and sometimes of poor quality; the tomb walls therefore had to be covered with plaster before they could be decorated.

EGYPT'S GOLDEN AGE

The New Kingdom is often called the Golden Age of Empire. This era of expansion began in the mid-16th century BC, when the 17th Dynasty Theban prince Ahmose succeeded in driving out the Hyksos – foreign chieftains who had occupied much of Egypt for the previous century – and founded the 18th Dynasty. He set in train several centuries of Egyptian imperialism by chasing the invaders into their homeland to the northeast and beginning to reclaim the Nubian lands to the south of Egypt, once controlled by the monarchs of the Middle Kingdom.

Ahmose also initiated what was to be a tradition for the next four centuries, of building monuments in the Theban area to honor Amun, a local god raised to prominence by the new king's 17th Dynasty ancestors. Merged with the sun god Re, Amun-Re became the head of the Egyptian pantheon. As each king made

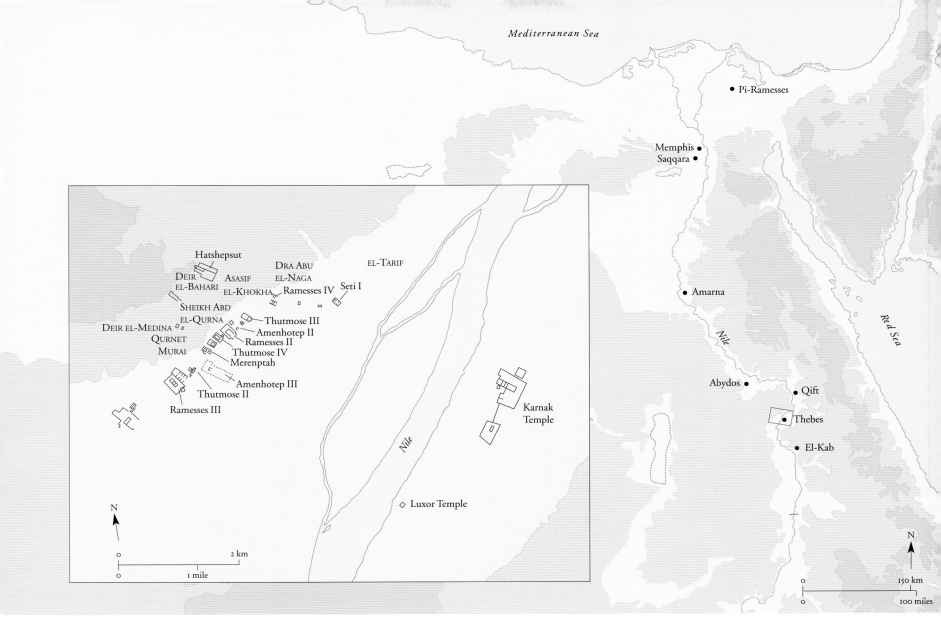

A map of Egypt with the main sites mentioned in the text; the inset shows the positions of the cemeteries on the West Bank of the Nile in relation to the memorial temples of various New Kingdom pharaohs. Courtiers and officials tended to build their tombs in proximity to the mortuary temple of the monarch under whom they had served.

offerings to the cult of this god as thanks for their victories abroad, the power and wealth of the Amun priesthood eventually came to rival that of the monarchy itself. For most of the New Kingdom Thebes remained the religious capital and one of the key political and administrative centers of the country. Many illustrious pharaohs ruled during this era, and were buried in the Theban hills, surrounded by the final resting places of their families, their courtiers, and their high officials. Some of the most famous monarchs of the 18th Dynasty are Hatshepsut, the female pharaoh who held power over the "Two Lands" (Upper and Lower Egypt) for two decades, and her stepson, Thutmose III, remembered as one of Egypt's greatest warriors. Thutmose III's great-grandson was Amenhotep III, the Sun King, who in turn engendered the "heretic pharaoh," Akhenaten. Ruling with his beautiful queen, Nefertiti, beside him, Akhenaten overturned the traditional religion of Egypt in favor of the Aten, the disk of the sun.

Akhenaten was, in all likelihood, the father of Egypt's most celebrated monarch: the boy-king Tutankhamun. Most people know only of this king's fabulous treasure discovered in his tomb, but before his death and burial he ruled for around 10 years during a period both of great change in Egypt and of chaos in the Near East in general. Tutankhamun and his two successors all died without issue, and the 18th Dynasty came to an end.

The 18th Dynasty is a period that I personally find fascinating. I currently direct the Egyptian Mummy Project, which uses cutting-edge technology to study ancient mummies. In 2006, we used a CT-scanner to examine the mummy of Tutankhamun, and proved that he had not been killed by a blow to the head, as some people had speculated. We confirmed that he had a recent break to his leg, indicating that he had probably had an accident shortly before he died. We are now also performing CT-scans and DNA analysis on the royal mummies from this era, hoping to learn more about Tutankhamun's family and answer questions about his parentage and ancestry. In 2008, in another study carried out by the Egyptian Mummy Project, we CT-scanned a group of anonymous royal female mummies from this era, and were able to identify the mummy of Hatshepsut (see p. 37).

The next dynasty, the 19th, was a vigorous line that originated in the Egyptian Delta. The most renowned of its kings was Ramesses II, known to posterity as Ramesses the Great. Under this long-lived and charismatic monarch, Egypt succeeded in retaining much of its original empire and also made peace with its most powerful foes to the northeast, the Hittites. These pharaohs built a new northern administrative center of the country in their Delta homeland, called Pi-Ramesses (modern Qantir).

One of the most interesting projects that I am currently undertaking is the restoration of the tunnel that begins in the burial chamber of Seti I – another of the distinguished pharaohs of the 19th Dynasty – in the Valley of the Kings. Thus far, we have penetrated 136 meters into the cliff, we have securing the ceiling with iron beams and installing 70 meters of wooden stairs and ramps. During our clearance of this mysterious tunnel, we found a number of interesting artifacts, including pottery, shabtis, a plaque bearing the cartouche of Seti, and what looks like a model of a small boat. We hope through our excavations here to learn whether this tunnel was built as a magical route to the mythical Cave of Osiris, or whether it leads to a secret burial chamber for Seti I.

The 20th Dynasty saw the end of Egyptian hegemony in the Near East. It was a time of major population movements around the Mediterranean, perhaps stimulated by climate change, and the rise of new superpowers. Eventually, the centralized monarchy collapsed, as the resources of the royal house were sapped and the High Priests of Amun at Thebes challenged royal authority. Soon after 1100 BC, the New Kingdom gave way to the instability of the Third Intermediate Period and the Golden Age came to an end.

THE TOMBS OF THE NOBLES

Built to serve as the eternal homes of the officials and nobles who were buried within them, the New Kingdom elite tombs at Thebes cover an area of approximately 9 square kilometers at the edge of the western high desert. Modern scholars have divided this swath of rocky land into six cemeteries, known collectively as the Valley of the Nobles. Farthest north is el-Tarif, where most of the tombs date to the Middle Kingdom and early Second Intermediate Period. To the south of el-Tarif is Dra Abu el-Naga. This was the burial place of the princes of the 17th Dynasty, the royal line that culminated in Ahmose. To the south and west, near the great memorial temple of Hatshepsut at Deir el-Bahari, is the Asasif, followed by el-Khokha. Many of the tombs that appear in this book are from the necropolis that lies south and west of el-Khokha. Called Sheikh Abd el-Qurna, it contains more than 140 tombs, primarily dating to the 18th Dynasty. The southernmost Theban elite private cemetery is Qurnet Murai. These necropolises were closely associated with the royal burial ground in the Valley of the Kings, and the royal memorial temples that lined the edge of the western floodplain. If possible, officials tended to place their tombs west of the temples of the monarchs they had attended in life and wished to serve after death.

West of Qurnet Murai, nestled high in the Theban hills, was a special community for the artisans who carved and decorated the tombs of the pharaohs. The eastern part of this site, called Deir el-Medina, is home to the walled town where the royal workmen and their families lived; on the rocky slopes to the west lie their tombs. Most of the extant tombs here date to the Ramesside era, and, as they

PAGES 16–18
The funeral cortege of the vizier Ramose, as depicted in great detail in his tomb (TT 55). Lines of mourners and offering bearers carrying burial equipment, furniture, and food and drink process to the tomb of this high-ranking official of the 18th Dynasty.

were built and decorated by the skilled artists responsible for the royal tombs (and probably many of the tombs of the high elite as well), they are themselves often wonderfully decorated and thus provide us with fascinating information that adds greatly to our understanding of Egyptian burial practices in the New Kingdom. Each documented tomb in these various cemeteries is given an individual number, preceded by the abbreviation TT, for Theban Tomb.

The tombs we explore and illustrate here cover the full span of the New Kingdom and include the final resting places of many of the most important players in the cosmopolitan world of the pharaohs. These include the viziers Rekhmire and Ramose, the army commander Amenemhab, who campaigned with some of the greatest warrior pharaohs and helped build the Egyptian empire, and the royal architect Ineni, who was responsible for hiding the tomb of Thutmose I in the Theban hills. Featured here also will be Senenmut, Chief Steward of Hatshepsut, as well as the High Priest of Amun, Menkheperreseneb, and a number of "Children of the Nursery" – men who were raised in the royal palace and became loyal officials of the kings alongside whom they had played as children. Their tombs exemplify the various architectural styles and developments of this period, and their superb decoration illuminates the various themes chosen by the tomb owners to commemorate their lives on earth and guarantee themselves a successful afterlife. Within these sacred spaces, the deceased were transformed into blessed spirits, able to live eternally in an ideal land beyond the earth. While the cult at each tomb was active, mortuary priests, as well as the relatives of the deceased, could come to make offerings and say prayers to their honored ancestors, and the tombs thus also served as liminal zones where the worlds of the living and the dead came together.

A view of the great bay of cliffs at Deir el-Bahari, with the memorial temple of the female pharaoh Hatshepsut in the background and private elite tombs carved into the hillside in the foreground.

Together, both the well-known and "lost" tombs that are explored in this book illuminate the earthly existence of the ancient Egyptians as well as the magical functions of these miniature temples for the cult of the dead. Some might say that they can also help us elucidate the history of Egypt during this extraordinary era. Chapter 1 begins by looking at the complex and evolving administration of the New Kingdom, and introduces some of the powerful nobles and officials whose tombs have been chosen for inclusion here. Each tomb owner will be placed in the context of the pharaoh under whom he served and the eventful times in which he lived. Chapter 2 reviews the architectural styles represented by these tombs. The New Kingdom tombs all follow a basic plan consisting of a cult chapel above and one or more burial chambers below; here the typical architectural components of each style and how they functioned in the tomb will be discussed.

At the heart of the book are several chapters on the superb decoration of the Theban private tombs. Detailed study of the tomb paintings in the Valley of the Nobles allows us to establish the techniques and principles used in creating these masterpieces, and even possibly to identify the hand of individual artists. Chapter 3 examines these questions and provides an introduction to the chapters that follow.

The paintings that cover the walls of each tomb, in most cases of the upper chapel only, but sometimes also of the burial suites, were planned and executed carefully. Chosen in advance by the tomb owner, these scenes were designed both

PAGES 19–21
This complex of scenes illustrating the various ceremonies that formed part of an elite New Kingdom funeral is from the tomb of the vizier Rekhmire (TT 100). It provides one of the fullest representations of the ideal funeral and its associated rituals, both on earth and in the divine realm.

The tomb owner, Suenmut (TT 92), is represented several times in this composition. On the left side, a cult celebrant makes offerings to the deceased and his wife; in front of them is a table piled high with various foodstuffs. On the right Suenmut appears twice in scenes of marsh hunts: fowling with a throwstick and spearing fish with a harpoon. The painting was never finished, and the underlying grid used to organize the scene and aid the artists in copying its elements onto the wall is still visible in places.

to honor and preserve the memory of the deceased among those still living, and to guarantee his or her successful transition to an eternal existence in the afterlife. As a result, the scenes and texts within these tombs, which vary over time and from tomb to tomb within a specific period, provide us with important information about both life on earth and the religious beliefs of the ancient Egyptians.

Chapter 4 is dedicated to depictions of "earthly life." Although these types of scenes serve specific magical functions within the context of the death and resurrection of the tomb owner, they also provide a window into the daily and official lives of the nobles and their families. Many tomb scenes show the deceased in relationship to the pharaoh, and also depict the activities for which the official was responsible during life. For example, a granary official might show scenes of agriculture, so that the process of preparing the soil, planting the grain, and harvesting the crops would be eternally under his competent supervision. A vizier might choose a scene of foreign tribute, providing us with information about the physical features, clothing, and typical trade goods of neighbors to the south, north, northeast, and west of Egypt. From the tomb of a military official might come depictions of army parades. For very special service to the king, an official might receive collars of gold in a public ceremony; this would certainly be represented on the walls of his tomb, to be repeated in perpetuity. Other scenes show "sporting" activities, such as hunting in the desert and fishing and fowling in the marshes; these also carry

The burial chamber of the royal artisan Nebenma'at, covered with scenes associated with the funeral and the eternal afterlife (TT 219). On the back wall, the mummy in its coffin lies on a table while a priest wearing the mask of the god Anubis leans over to perform the Opening of the Mouth ceremony.

significant ritual overtones, representing at one level the triumph of the proper order of the Egyptian world over the chaos that was believed to surround and threaten it.

Many of the scenes found in the tombs illustrate the transition to, and life in, the world beyond, and these are the subject of Chapter 5. Seen here, for example, are images connected with the funeral, including the rituals carried out in front of the tomb itself. Among the other scene types covered in the chapter are images of purification rites, pilgrimages to various sacred cult sites, and the meeting of the deceased with the gods. Also included are images from religious texts such as the *Book of Coming Forth by Day*, commonly known as the *Book of the Dead*.

Scenes depicting the presentation of offerings were essential for making sure that the deceased was provided with a perpetual supply of food and drink; these are described and discussed Chapter 6. At the center of such scenes are images of the tomb owner and his family seated at tables piled high with fabulous comestibles. Surrounding these core icons, which date back to the beginning of Egyptian history, are often rows and rows of offering bearers, as well as relatives performing the cult. An extension of the offering meal is the banqueting scene, also covered in Chapter 6.

In addition to the scenes painted on the walls of the tombs, various objects were deposited in the tomb to accompany the deceased for use of the deceased in the Netherworld. Although the vast majority of the equipment buried with the New Kingdom elite at Thebes has been removed by robbers over the centuries, enough remains to give Egyptologists a good idea of the items that the Egyptians considered necessary for the afterlife. Chapter 7 will review these objects, and explain how they were meant to help ensure, or be used in, the eternal life of the deceased.

The fate of the Theban tombs after the New Kingdom is the subject of Chapter 8. Unfortunately, as noted, the tombs of the nobles, like the burials of their kings, were frequently robbed in antiquity and almost every tomb that was not plundered in ancient times has been violated in the modern era. Only a few tombs have survived intact to be excavated by archaeologists, although even the robbed tombs have stories to tell to the expert eye. Modern pressures and external factors such as tourism and neglect threaten these tombs today, and without a major campaign to save the Valley of the Nobles, many of these tombs will be completely destroyed by the end of this century or even sooner. Chapter 9 discusses the current and recent archaeological missions working in the Theban necropolis, and also focuses on the efforts of the Supreme Council of Antiquities, with the support of our Egyptian and foreign colleagues, to preserve what remains.

This book is richly illustrated with superb and highly detailed photographs by Sandro Vannini. Covering both tombs that are open and well-known to the public and those that have been closed for decades to all but scholars, these images serve as an important record of these irreplaceable monuments and help to illuminate the world of the ancient Egyptians. In this volume, the reader is invited not only to learn about the known and "lost" tombs of New Kingdom Thebes, but also to join in the adventure of saving this great heritage for future generations.

The god Osiris seated before the Western Mountain, from the tomb of a royal artisan, Pashedu, at Deir el-Medina (TT 3). Behind Osiris, the *wedjat* eye of the sky god Horus holds a burning torch, while Pashedu kneels below. Some of the most interesting Theban tombs are found at Deir el-Medina; the majority date to the Ramesside era, and include beautifully decorated burial chambers, their walls and barrel-vaulted ceilings covered with interwoven scenes.

CHAPTER ONE
THE NOBLES OF THE NEW KINGDOM AT THEBES

Vizier, Counter of the Grain of Amun, Overseer of All the King's Work, Child of the Nursery – who were the people behind these grand titles? The lives of the elite, as revealed to us in large part through the scenes adorning their tombs, also tell the history of the age of power and glory that was New Kingdom Egypt. Such scenes provide insight into the daily existence and official functions of viziers, viceroys, treasury administrators, high priests, granary supervisors, royal stewards, tutors, and nurses, and other officials from the Egyptian court: the men and women who stood behind the pharaohs of the Golden Age of Egypt. This chapter will introduce the owners of the tombs featured here and will place them in their historical context.

The population of New Kingdom Egypt has been estimated at about 3 million, the majority living in villages along the narrow strip of flood-plain that bordered the Nile and in the wide, fertile Delta to the north. The largest concentrations of people would have been in cult and administrative centers such as Thebes and Memphis, and later Pi-Ramesses, which were most likely the size of today's small cities.

Officially, most land was either held by the crown or belonged to divine temples, but there were also privately owned fields, bestowed as rewards for service to king or god. Most Egyptians would have been farmers of various classes, ranging from wealthy estate-holders to peasants and slaves who worked the land of others. A number of other professions are known as well, as graphically illustrated in the tombs: pastoralists who herded cattle or other animals; bakers and brewers; artisans who carved and painted statues and tombs; carpenters who manufactured furniture and funerary goods; weavers; jewelers; soldiers; and scribes. Overseeing this complex society was a well-developed administration answering directly to the king, who in turn was responsible for carrying out the will of the gods.

THE ADMINISTRATION OF THE NEW KINGDOM
THE AHMOSIDS (C. 1539–1493 BC)
In the mid-16th century BC Ahmose, scion of the Theban 17th Dynasty, expelled the Hyksos from Egypt and reunited the country, ending the Second Intermediate Period and establishing the 18th Dynasty. After the final battle on Egyptian soil, the new king pursued his advantage by chasing his foreign foes into southern Palestine, laying the foundation for what would become a vast northern empire. To the south, he fought the kings of Kush and completed the reclamation of Lower Nubia, which had been Egyptian territory during the Middle Kingdom. Ahmose's son and successor, Amenhotep I, continued his father's policies.

A strong, centralized Egyptian bureaucracy that could exert control over all Egypt was reinstated and reorganized by Ahmose and Amenhotep I. The principal aims of the royal administration were threefold: to collect revenue; organize the labor force for major projects; and to maintain the basic social and political order.

These two scene complexes come from the tomb of Amenemhat (TT 82), who bore the titles of Scribe, Counter of the Grain of Amun, and Steward of the Vizier under Thutmose III. Above is the funerary procession, along with the pilgrimage to Abydos; below, Amenemhat and his friends enjoy a banquet, attended by servants and entertained by a small musical troupe.

PAGES 31–33
Various scenes from the funeral celebrations of Rekhmire, Vizier under Thutmose III and Amenhotep II. The god of embalming, Anubis, stands at the right, receiving offerings (TT 100).

Apart from the obvious practical benefits of the system in terms of both increasing wealth and providing a safety net for the people, this bureaucracy also served to assist the king in fulfilling his essential function of placating and caring for the gods. Controlling foreign vassals to the north and managing the lands to the south also required well-developed bureaucracies, albeit ones closely connected to the central administration.

Although we have few Theban tombs from the first reigns of the 18th Dynasty, other sources, including inscribed stelae set up in temples and information from several important tombs to the south at El-Kab, provide us with some of the details of Ahmose's and Amenhotep I's bureaucracy, which followed the basic patterns set in earlier eras. This, coupled with information from later reigns, allows us to reconstruct, to some extent, the structure of the hierarchy for the administration of New Kingdom Egypt. There were certainly changes over time, and the precise duties performed by the holders of the individual offices could be flexible. One person might also hold multiple offices, and even serve different departments, such as the state and the temple, at the same time.

The New Kingdom bureaucracy can be divided roughly into four parts: the state and palace; the military; regional government; and the administration of the divine cults. Many offices were split and held simultaneously by two people, one for the north of Egypt and the other for the south. The highest state officers were the two viziers (ancient Egyptian *tjaty*), who were second only to the king himself. For most of the New Kingdom, the northern Vizier was based at Memphis, and the southern one at Thebes; during the Ramesside period, the northern seat moved to Pi-Ramesses (now Qantir) in the eastern Delta.

The niched and carved façade of the tomb of Useramun (TT 131), Vizier and Governor of the Town under Thutmose III; Useramun also had a second tomb (TT 61). High officials would be granted the honor of a burial place in the Valley of the Nobles by their pharaoh.

Next in order of importance came the two Overseers of the Seal and the Overseers of the Granary, followed by the Overseers of the Gold and Silver Houses (the Treasury), the Overseer of the Gate, and the Royal Heralds and Messengers, who also served the palace (as, in reality, did all state officials). These officials were supported by a multiplicity of lower-ranking functionaries.

The palace administration was headed by the king's Chief Steward, followed by the Royal Butler Clean of Hands. Also high in the palace ranking were the Children of the Nursery, whose functions are unclear but who seem to have been brought up with the royal princes, and the Royal Nurse. At the head of the military was the Overseer (Commander-in-Chief) of the Army; while the country's regional administration was managed by a series of mayors. The Nubian empire was governed by a Viceroy (whose title translates literally as "King's Son of Kush").

With the Theban line now in the ascendancy, Amun, the local deity of Thebes, became the principal state god of New Kingdom Egypt. The kings offered much of the booty resulting from their foreign wars to the cult of Amun, constructing monuments in his honor and adding treasure, land, and personnel to his holdings. A large and complex bureaucracy was required to oversee such wealth and property, and similar administrations were put in place for the cults of the other major Egyptian gods. Many high officials of the early 18th Dynasty served both the king and the gods, especially Amun. The High Priest of Amun was one of the highest officials in the land.

It was the holders of these offices, and those in the next ranks down, who were rewarded by their monarchs with the privilege of burial in the Valley of the Nobles. Their tombs, even though most were robbed and some were usurped by later bureaucrats or other inhabitants of the area, can thus provide us with remarkable details about many of the highest officials of New Kingdom Egypt. The texts (including some "autobiographies") and scenes in the tombs illuminate the society in which these men and their families lived, and even, in some cases, bring to light historical information not available elsewhere.

THE THUTMOSIDS (C. 1493–1322 BC)

The direct Ahmosid line died with Amenhotep I, and the Egyptian throne passed to an army general named Thutmose I, who is believed to have been married to an Ahmosid princess. Thutmose I was a vigorous campaigner and marched the armies of Egypt as far as the Euphrates in the northeast, where he faced and defeated the dominant superpower of the region, the Mitanni; in the south, he reached the Fourth Cataract. The northern military campaigns seem to have been more in the nature of sorties, in which muscles were flexed and booty collected, rather than full-scale invasions intended to establish new boundaries for the empire. Thutmose I was also active within Egypt's borders, erecting monuments at many sites, including the Temple of Karnak.

One of the most interesting of the Theban tombs of Thutmose I's reign belongs to a Royal Architect and Overseer of the Granary of Amun named Ineni (TT 81). Ineni served under Amenhotep I, rose to prominence under Thutmose I, and continued his career under the next three kings. In the autobiography carved on a stela in the portico of his little-known tomb chapel, he describes how he hid the tomb of Thutmose I in the Theban hills, "no one seeing and no one hearing." The workforce he used for this endeavor would have come from Deir el-Medina, where Thutmose I founded, or reorganized, a community of royal artisans responsible for building the royal tombs.

Another important official of this king's reign was Turi, Viceroy of Nubia, who left his name on several monuments, but whose tomb has not yet been identified. There are at least 11 known tombs at Thebes belonging to military officers

Benia Pakhamun, Overseer of Works and Child of the Nursery in the early 18th Dynasty, supervises the bringing of gold and other goods to be weighed and recorded by scribes (TT 343).

who served under Thutmose I, demonstrating the increasing importance of the military elite. One of the "lost" tombs of this period belongs to Benia Pakhamun (TT 343), who was an Overseer of Works and a Child of the Nursery from the early 18th Dynasty. We know from Benia's titles that he was brought up in the royal harem, alongside a future king, and remained high in royal favor during his lifetime.

Egyptian queens had always been essential to the success of the royal house, and played important ritual roles in the royal and divine cults. Although prior to the New Kingdom true political power was wielded by only a few royal women, the 17th Dynasty was distinguished by its strong matriarchs. Ahmose's mother, Ahhotep, is believed to have acted as regent during her son's minority. She may perhaps even have led the Theban armies into battle. Ahmose's great queen, Ahmose-Nefertari (who was probably his full sister too) was the first to hold the important title Divine Wife of Amun, and perhaps in addition was the Second Priest of Amun. It is certain that she held significant power in both the religious and political realms.

Thutmose I's throne had probably been secured by his marriage to a princess Ahmose, who was the next Divine Wife of Amun. She in turn passed this title to her eldest daughter, Hatshepsut, who was also the Great Royal Wife of Thutmose II, Thutmose I's eldest son, but by a minor queen. Thutmose II died after about a dozen years of rule, and was succeeded by the young son he had begotten with a secondary queen named Isis. Since this king, Thutmose III, was still only a child, his aunt (who was also his stepmother), Hatshepsut became regent. Perhaps seven years into Thutmose III's reign, this powerful queen took on the full titulary of a pharaoh and joined her stepson on the throne.

Hatshepsut's most valued official was her Chief Steward, Senenmut, who had begun his career under Thutmose II. From the town of Armant south of Thebes, he was of humble birth and seems to have risen to prominence on his own merit. Long rumored (with no solid evidence) to be the pharaoh-queen's lover, Senenmut was appointed nurse/tutor to Hatshepsut's daughter with Thutmose II, Neferure, and is credited with supervising the building of the queen's great memorial temple at Deir el-Bahari.

Senenmut, Chief Steward of the female pharaoh Hatshepsut, had two tombs. Above, from TT 71, are several of his titles, the hieroglyphs carved in relief and painted blue; on the right is a sketch labeled as "Steward of Amun, Senenmut," from TT 353, close to Hatshepsut's memorial temple at Deir el-Bahari, where he was buried.

It is instructive to look at Senenmut's career: his titulary tells us that he was appointed to over 50 offices, representing the many supervisory roles that he filled. Among the tasks he was charged with was the quarrying at Aswan of monolithic obelisks for the glory of both Amun and his queen, and organizing a major trading expedition to Punt (probably in modern Sudan or Eritrea), to bring back luxury goods such as incense trees. At Sheikh Abd el-Qurna, TT 71, which is closed to the public and unknown to most people, was built and decorated for Senenmut, but only his chapel is here. He was honored with burial near his monarch's temple, in an exquisite subterranean chamber with carved decoration (TT 353).

There are many other tombs from the reign of Hatshepsut clustered at Sheikh Abd el-Qurna. Another of her key officials was Hapuseneb (TT 67), who was Vizier and High Priest of Amun as well as Overseer of All the King's Work and Keeper of the Seal of Lower Egypt, demonstrating the overlap of major royal and priestly duties that was common during this era. Hapuseneb's father, Hapu, had been a lesser Priest of Amun, and his mother, Ahhotep, was a royal concubine who may have been connected with the 17th Dynasty. The surviving decoration in Hapuseneb's tomb indicates that he too was involved with the Punt expedition, and he is also credited with supervising the construction of his monarch's tomb in the Valley of the Kings. The tomb of Duaneheh (TT 125), whose principal titles were First Royal Herald and Overseer of the Estate of Amun, is closed to the public and contains some unfamiliar but fascinating scenes.

Hatshepsut disappears from the historical record after about 20 years on the throne. My forensic team and I recently carried out a "search" for this queen, using a state-of-the-art CT-scanner. We were able to match a tooth contained in a wooden box labeled with Hatshepsut's cartouches to her mummy – we had found Hatshepsut. The CT-scan also showed that she died of cancer at about the age of 50. After her death, Thutmose III came into his own. At some point in his reign, he ordered that the name and image of his stepmother be erased from many of her monuments, which was once was taken as evidence that he hated her, and perhaps even had her murdered. However, it is now clear that this *damnatio memoriae*, perhaps a political necessity due to the fact that the rule of a female pharaoh was against the basic rules of Egyptian kingship, took place at the end of his reign, probably when he raised his son Amenhotep II to sit beside him on the throne.

Remembered by history as a great warrior king, Thutmose III began his sole reign by marching the Egyptian army to Megiddo, in ancient Palestine, where he defeated a coalition of Syro-Palestinian city-states who were threatening Egyptian hegemony in the region. The strategy he used to win this victory – taking the most dangerous and unexpected route to attack the enemy – is still taught in military academies today. He continued to campaign to the northeast, extending Egypt's empire of vassal states north to the Euphrates and inland to Qadesh. He also married at least three Syrian princesses, whose shared tomb was discovered hidden in the Theban hills. To the south, Thutmose III and his well-trained troops secured the Nubian empire as far as the Fourth Cataract.

Officials of the reign of Thutmose III are well represented in the Theban necropolis, again mainly in the Sheikh Abd el-Qurna region. The continuity of the administration from the reigns of Thutmose I through Thutmose III is illustrated by the family of the vizier Ametju (Ahmose), whose mother, named Ahhotep, may have had some connection to the Ahmosid line. Ametju, buried in TT 83, was succeeded by his son, Useramun, who had two tombs, TT 61 and TT 131. Both father and son also held the title Governor of the Town (Mayor). Useramun was in turn succeeded by his nephew Rekhmire (TT 100; see below). Ametju is mentioned or

The cult shrine, with rock-cut statues of the tomb owner and his family, from the tomb of Duaneheh, First Royal Herald and Overseer of the Estate of Amun under Hatshepsut (TT 125).

represented in a number of other tombs, and there is an unusual scene in the tomb of his grandson Rekhmire, depicting a gallery of ancestors.

The next level of the bureaucracy is represented by a Steward of the Vizier, Amenemhat (TT 82), who also held the titles of Scribe and Counter of the Grain of Amun, again illustrating the overlap of royal and priestly duties during this era. The High Priest of Amun, Menkheperreseneb, who was the son of a royal nurse, had two tombs (TT 86 and TT 112), demonstrating the importance of his position. It is interesting to note that the tomb of Menkheperreseneb's second-in-command, the Second Priest of Amun Puemre (TT 39), which lies at el-Khokha, is extremely large and extensively decorated.

Tombs belonging to the military serving under Thutmose III are also found in the Valley of the Nobles. One army commander, Amenemhab (TT 85), is well known to Egyptologists because of his tomb biography, in which he reports that after their successful eighth campaign into Asia Minor, the king undertook a major elephant hunt, killing 120 animals for their tusks. Amenemhab saved his monarch by cutting off the "hand" (presumably the trunk) of an attacking elephant, and was rewarded for this act of valor with the gold of honor. The decoration of this tomb is little-known, but includes some interesting and even unique scenes. Another important official was the Royal Herald Yamunedjeh (TT 84), who also accompanied his monarch on campaign to Asia Minor.

As noted above, toward the end of his long and illustrious reign, Thutmose III raised his son, Amenhotep II, to join him on the throne as co-regent. After his father's death, the new pharaoh continued to carry out building projects, especially in the Theban area, and is known to have undertaken at least two campaigns to the northeast. Exceedingly proud of his prowess as a sportsman and warrior, Amenhotep II enjoyed hunting in the desert near Giza, and built a small temple to the Great Sphinx as an incarnation of the sun god there.

One of the most impressively decorated tombs in the entire Theban necropolis, TT 100, belongs to Rekhmire, who became southern Vizier and Governor of the Town (Mayor of Thebes) under Thutmose III, and continued to occupy these positions during the reign of Amenhotep II. Other officials whose careers spanned the reigns of these two kings include Menkheper, an Overseer of the Granary of the Lord of the Two Lands and Purification Priest in the mortuary temple of Thutmose III (TT 79), who inherited this position from his father, Nakhtmin (TT 87), and another career military man, Pekhsukher Tjenenu. Lieutenant of the King and Standard-bearer of the Lord of the Two Lands, Pekhsukher Tjenenu was married to a Chief Royal Nurse and Governess of the god named Neith, a fact that may have helped earn him the right to an elaborate burial (TT 88).

Rekhmire was followed as southern Vizier by Amenemopet Pairy (TT 29), who was awarded the great honor of a second tomb in the Valley of the Kings (KV 48). Other royal officials buried at Thebes whose tombs are featured here include the Child of the Nursery and Royal Scribe, Userhat (TT 56); Child of the Nursery and Royal Archer, Paser (TT 367); Royal Scribe and Overseer of the Treasury, Djehutynefer (TT 80); and a palace official named Suenmut with the title of Royal Butler Clean of Hands (TT 92). Rivaling and perhaps even surpassing the slightly earlier tomb of Rekhmire is the burial complex of Sennefer (TT 96), which is also distinguished by the fact that its burial chamber is extensively decorated, whereas in most tombs of the 18th Dynasty decoration was restricted to the upper chapel.

The next ruler, Thutmose IV, was evidently one of a number of sons of Amenhotep II who aspired to the throne. He left a granite stela between the paws of the Great Sphinx on which he recorded the story of how, while still a prince, he had been hunting nearby and had fallen asleep in the shade of the statue's head. The Sphinx came to him in a dream and told him that if he would clear the sand away from its body, it would make him king. Some believe that this prince killed his

These two images from the burial chamber of TT 96 show Sennefer, who bore the title Mayor of the Southern City (Thebes) under Amenhotep II, attended by a female relative. Sennefer's tomb is unusual in having a decorated burial chamber – in most 18th Dynasty tombs the decoration was restricted to the upper chapel.

elder brother, the heir apparent, and that this stela was set up as propaganda to justify his reign. At this time the political landscape of the Near East was changing: after one recorded campaign into what is now Syria, Thutmose IV chose diplomacy rather than warfare, and married a princess of Egypt's most powerful rivals, the Mitanni.

Although Thutmose IV's reign saw fewer foreign campaigns, and forays into Nubia were no more than police actions, a military elite was now a fixed part of Egyptian society, and a number of army officers were granted tombs in the Theban necropolis. These include several little-known chapels, for instance those of Tjanuny, a Commander of Soldiers (TT 74); Horemheb, a Royal Scribe and Scribe of Recruits who had begun his career under Amenhotep II (TT 78); and Nebamun, Standard-bearer of "Beloved of Amun" (a sacred bark) and Captain of Troops of the Police on the West of Thebes (TT 90). Other interesting burials from this reign are TT 66, belonging to the vizier Hepu; the beautifully decorated and well-known tomb of Menna, who bore the title Scribe of the Fields of the Lord of the Two Lands of Upper and Lower Egypt (TT 69); and, representing the divine realm, the tomb of Amenhotep-si-se, the Second Priest of Amun (TT 75). Two small tombs that span this reign and the next are TT 116, constructed for an anonymous "Hereditary Prince," and TT 176, for a Servant Clean of Hands named Amenuserhat. Also

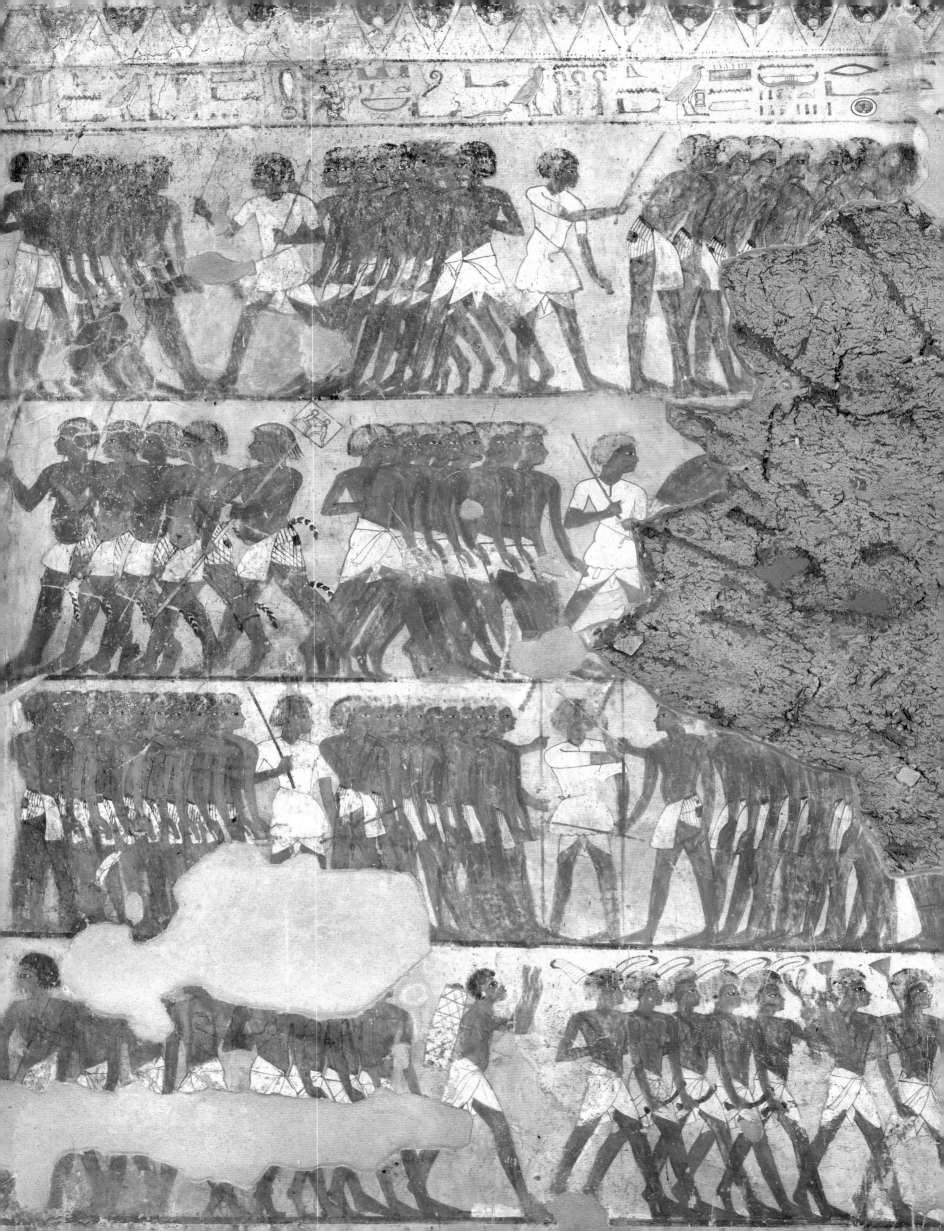

A military parade in several registers, with groups of soldiers bearing different weapons and insignia and marching under the watchful eye of officers, from the tomb of Tjanuny, Commander of Soldiers under Thutmose IV (TT 74).

possibly dating to the reign of Thutmose IV is TT 249, of Neferrenpet, who bore the relatively lowly title of Supplier of Dates/Cakes in the Temple of Amenhotep.

It is from this reign also that we have one of the earliest surviving tombs from the workmen's village at Deir el-Medina, belonging to the Chief of the Great Place, Kha (TT 8). Little decoration survives from this chapel, but the burial equipment was found intact, and can now be seen in the Egyptian Museum, Turin (see Chapter 7).

The long reign of Thutmose IV's son and successor, Amenhotep III, was an era of wealth and luxury that has been compared to the rule of France's "Sun King," Louis XIV. Egypt's coffers were full and the region was temporarily at peace. Art began to take on a new freedom, and innovation – in some cases disguised as the desire to reconstruct ancient ways – seems to have been encouraged. The rise of the sun cult, which had begun under Amenhotep II, gained momentum, to culminate

Attendants fan a figure of the king (of whom only the feet are visible here) in the tomb of Horemheb, a Royal Scribe and Scribe of Recruits during the reigns of Thutmose III through Amenhotep III (TT 78).

in the religious revolution of Amenhotep III's son, Amenhotep IV/Akhenaten. With his Great Royal Wife, Tiye, at his side, Amenhotep III undertook many ambitious building programs, including an enormous memorial temple on the West Bank of Thebes; virtually all that now remains of this are the two giant statues known as the Colossi of Memnon. Many of Amenhotep's officials were awarded burial in the Valley of the Nobles.

The area of Qurnet Murai was first used as a cemetery during Amenhotep's reign. Tombs from this era are also found on the lower slopes of Sheikh Abd el-

BELOW
Dancers representing the twin Delta cities of Dep and Pe perform a ritual fight with staffs in the shape of marsh plants during the celebration of the jubilee festival of Amenhotep III, from the tomb of Kheruef, Steward of the king's Great Royal Wife, Tiye (TT 192).

OVERLEAF
An exquisitely fine relief carving of Ramose, Vizier and
Governor of the Town under Amenhotep IV/Akhenaten,
and his wife, Merytptah, at the cult banquet (TT 55); both are
wearing intricate wigs.

Qurna, most likely placed here both because the upper slopes were becoming increasingly crowded and also because the better quality of the rock supported larger tombs and carved decoration. Several tombs from this reign, most of which are not well known to the general public, are seen here, including that of Amenmesse (TT 89), who was a Steward in the Southern City (Thebes). Beautiful scenes adorn the tomb of Pairy (TT 139), who bore the unusual titles of Priest in Front and First Royal Son in Front of Amun. One of the most elegantly decorated tombs, well known but not often visited, belongs to Kheruef (TT 192), Steward of Queen Tiye.

Also dating from this reign is the tomb of Tiye's parents, Yuya and Tjuya, who were honored with burial in the Valley of the Kings (KV 46), consisting only of their undecorated burial chamber (their as-yet undiscovered chapel was most probably elsewhere in the Theban hills). Substantially intact, this has yielded a great deal of information about the proper equipment for the elite tomb (see Chapter 7).

Spanning this reign and the early part of the next are the recently conserved tomb of Queen Tiye's brother, Anen, who was the Second Priest of Amun (TT 120); and one of the best-known and most important monuments in the area, the unfinished tomb of Ramose (TT 55). Another interesting tomb from the Amenhotep III to Amenhotep IV period is that of Nebamun (TT 181), Chief Sculptor of the Lord of the Two Lands, who shared his tomb with his brother Ipuky, also a royal sculptor. The prominence given to these two men attests to the importance of art during this era.

Amenhotep III and Tiye's eldest surviving son began his reign at Thebes under the name Amenhotep IV, but soon changed it to Akhenaten. He also began construction of a new capital at what is now known as Amarna, halfway between Thebes and Memphis, dedicated to the worship of the disk of the sun, the Aten. Many of his high officials followed the royal family and built tombs at Amarna, so the Theban area saw little tomb construction. Tutankhamun, most likely Akhenaten's son, brought the court back to Thebes, but reigned for only 10 years; a number of his high officials were buried at Saqqara.

Tutankhamun died without an heir, and his successor, an elderly army officer named Ay (probably another brother of Queen Tiye), ruled for a very short time. He was succeeded in turn by Tutankhamun's Commander-in-Chief, Horemheb, who ruled for many years and completed the process begun by the boy-king of renewing the cults of the state gods that had been closed and stripped of their

The mummies of Nebamun and Ipuky stand in front of their tomb, as funerary rites are performed for them (TT 181). These two royal sculptors lived during the reigns of Amenhotep III and his son, Amenhotep IV/Akhenaten.

wealth by Akhenaten. A late 18th Dynasty tomb featured here belongs to two Deir el-Medina artisans, the Servant in the Great Place, Nu, and his brother, the Servant in the Place of Truth, Nakhtmin (TT 291).

Horemheb was faced with a new enemy in Egypt's northern protectorates: the Hittites. From their stronghold in central Anatolia, these Indo-European warriors had begun to build an empire, eventually toppling the Mitanni and upsetting the balance of power in the region. The Hittites had first emerged as a rival to Egypt's hegemony in the northeast during the reign of Akhenaten, and had already taken control of some of Egypt's northern empire. Hittite sources tell us that Egypt tried to recover some of its lost territories, but Horemheb was apparently merely fighting a holding action. He had no living heir, and so, perhaps in response to the delicate political situation abroad and his own military background, he appointed an army commander named Paramesse to succeed him on the throne.

THE 19TH AND 20TH DYNASTIES (c. 1292–1069 BC)

Paramesse became Ramesses I, inaugurating the 19th Dynasty. He was succeeded by his son, Seti I, and then his grandson, Ramesses II (the Great), both warrior kings. They maintained a firm grip on the Nubian empire and struggled to win back Egypt's Near Eastern vassal states, clashing frequently with the Hittites. Although he was renowned for his military prowess, as well as his great personal bravery and strength, Ramesses II was also a canny diplomat. With population movements and new powers threatening the established order in the region, both he and the Hittite king realized that they could not continue to fight one another. In about 1260 BC, they signed the first known peace treaty, and Ramesses II married at least one Hittite princess to seal the accord. True heirs to the traditions of the New Kingdom, the early Ramessides continued to worship the great god Amun-Re and build monuments in his honor. They moved the political capital of the country from Memphis to their family seat in the Delta, building a new city at Pi-Ramesses (Qantir).

A number of tombs from the reigns of Seti I and his son are in general not as well known as their 18th Dynasty counterparts. Decorated with wonderful carvings, although left largely unfinished, was the tomb of their Vizier and Governor of the Town, Paser (TT 106). Some other officials from this era bore religious titles related to both the cult of Amun and to the mortuary cults of the pharaohs. Neferhotep (TT 49) was Chief Scribe of Amun, while the little-known but important TT 178 at el-Khokha belonged to Neferrenpet, Scribe of the Treasury in the Estate of Amun-Re. Piay (TT 263) was a Granary Scribe in the Domain of Amun, and Huy (TT 54), who had begun his career in the late 18th Dynasty, was a sculptor of Amun and a priest. Other beautiful "lost" tombs are those of Userhat (TT 51) and Khonsu (TT 31), High Priest of the Royal *Ka* of Thutmose I and First Priest of Thutmose III, respectively; and Nakhtamun (TT 341), Chief of the Altar in the Ramesseum (the mortuary temple of Ramesses II). A small tomb at el-Khokha, TT 177, belonged to a Scribe of Truth in the Ramesseum in the Estate of Amun named Amenemopet.

There is an increase in the number of preserved decorated tombs at Deir el-Medina from the early 19th Dynasty, including that of the Foreman Neferhotep (TT 216). Few people visit the tomb of Ipuy (TT 217), a sculptor, but it contains fascinating scenes. One of the most famous tombs at Deir el-Medina, and the one visited by most tourists, belonged to Sennedjem, a Servant in the Place of Truth who lived during the reign of Ramesses II. The first tomb studied in the Valley of the Nobles in modern times, this bears the identifying number TT 1.

After an exceptional reign of 67 years, during which time he is thought to have fathered over 100 children and had 8 different wives, Ramesses was succeeded by his 13th son, Merenptah. New difficulties threatened the Egyptians from abroad: the Libyans to the west attempted to invade the Delta, and population movements around the Mediterranean basin displaced a number of populations, who then banded together (and at some points allied themselves with the Libyans) to attack Egypt in their search for new lands to settle. A number of short reigns ended the 19th Dynasty, and the next great king was Ramesses III, second king of the 20th Dynasty. Successful at keeping the Libyans and the displaced Peoples of the Sea at bay, this pharaoh was not so fortunate at home, and appears to have been assassinated in a palace conspiracy, although he seems to have survived long enough both to try and to convict his murderers. Like his predecessors, Ramesses III continued to undertake important building projects, and Egypt, although increasingly beleaguered, was still able to maintain parts of its empire. However, pharaohs Ramesses IV through Ramesses XI gradually lost ground both at home and abroad, and soon after 1100 BC, the New Kingdom came to an end.

There are in general fewer large tombs of the elite at Thebes after the reign of Merenptah, perhaps due in part to the shift of power to the north with the move of the Ramesside capital to the Delta. In the 20th Dynasty, it was also a consequence of the steadily decreasing resources available for the building of private tombs. Texts from this era provide information about workmen's strikes and security problems caused by bands of marauding Libyans, painting a picture of a world in decay.

Representing the late 19th and early 20th Dynasty are the tombs of Khonsumes (TT 30), Scribe of the Treasury in the Estate of Amun-Re; Ameneminet (TT 277), Priest, Lector, Divine Father in the Mansion of Amenhotep III, at Qurnet Murai; Amenemhab (TT 278), Herdsman of Amun-Re; and Amenwahsu (TT 111), Scribe of the God's Writings in the Amun Domain. From the 20th Dynasty come the tombs of Imisibe (TT 65, usurped from Nebamun), Chief of the Temple Scribes in the Estate of Amun; and the oft-visited tomb of Shuroy (TT 13), Chief of the Brazier-bearers of Amun, at Dra Abu el-Naga.

Piay, Granary Scribe in the Domain of Amun during the reign of Ramesses II, and his wife raise their arms in adoration before a hymn to the composite sun god Amun-Re-Horakhty (TT 263).

OPPOSITE
The figure of Paser, Vizier and Governor of the Town under Seti I and his son Ramesses II, holding a staff; a hymn to Re is carved above and around him (TT 106).

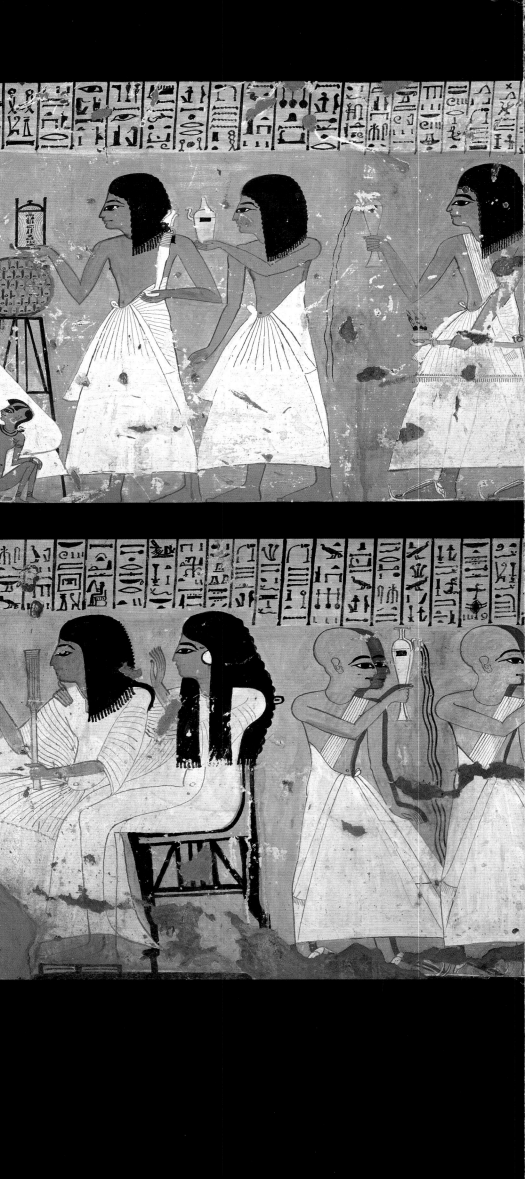

Isis and Nephthys attend to a figure of the deceased as an amalgamation of Re and Osiris, in the burial chamber of Nakhtamun, priest of Amenhotep I in the community of royal workmen at Deir el-Medina (TT 335).

Thoth and Harsiese (Horus, son of Isis), pour libations over the royal artisan Neferabet in this scene from his tomb at Deir el-Medina (TT 5).

A number of the most interesting tombs were carved and decorated at Deir el-Medina during the 19th and 20th Dynasties. Pashedu (TT 3), Neferabet (TT 5), and Irunefer (TT 290) were Servants in the Place of Truth (royal artisans). Spanning two generations, the tomb complex that includes TT 218, TT 219, and TT 220 was used for the burials of the Servant in the Place of Truth on the West of Thebes, Amennakht, and his sons, Nebenma'at and Khaemteri. The tomb numbered TT 335 was built for Nakhtamun, who was Purification Priest of Amenhotep I, Lord of the Two Lands (the "patron saint" of Deir el-Medina). One of the most beautiful tombs at Deir el-Medina, that of the Foreman in the Place of Truth, Inerkhau (TT 359), dates from the reign of Ramesses III and IV.

When the High Priests of Amun took control of the Theban region at the end of the 20th Dynasty, issues of security led them to bury their dead in hidden family tombs. During the Third Intermediate Period, such family caches, along with extensive reuse of earlier tombs, were the norm. It was not until the Late Period that large decorated tomb chapels appeared once again in the Theban necropolis. By the time the Romans conquered Egypt in 30 BC, most of the tombs of the New Kingdom had been robbed and many had also been vandalized. The great days of the Theban necropolis had come to an end.

A view of the upper burial chamber of Neferabet (TT 5) at Deir el-Medina, with the doorway into the lower chamber visible in the background. The precise architectural form of New Kingdom private tombs varies, but they all follow a basic plan consisting of a cult chapel above and one or more burial chambers below.

CHAPTER TWO

THE FUNCTION AND ARCHITECTURE OF THE THEBAN TOMBS

The study of the tombs of the nobles and officials of the New Kingdom provides us with useful information about mortuary architecture and its function, and can enlarge our knowledge of the Golden Age of Egypt. It is important to understand the concepts of death and the afterlife in the Egyptian worldview, and to see how these beliefs helped to form pharaonic civilization. From the late Predynastic period to the end of the pharaonic era, the ancient Egyptians lavished great care and attention on their burials, pouring enormous wealth into their construction and decoration. While we have little hard data to tell us exactly how the process worked, we can imagine that at some point in his career, an official was granted permission to build a tomb in the Valley of the Nobles. In some cases, it seems as if the royal artisans who carved and decorated the tombs in the Valley of the Kings worked on nobles' tombs as well. We do not know exactly how long it took to complete a tomb, but the fact that many burials took place in unfinished sepulchers suggests that construction was often begun not long before the death of the owner.

Although their architectural forms varied over time and from site to site, each tomb was carefully designed as an eternal dwelling for the deceased, where the earthly life of the tomb owner was commemorated and the safe transition of the soul from this world to the next was magically guaranteed. The body was housed for eternity in the subterranean chambers, and offerings were made and rituals performed in the upper chapel. The elite tomb can be seen, in essence, as a miniature temple where the deceased was perpetually transfigured, sustained, and worshipped as a divine being. Like gods' temples, some tombs could function as models of the Egyptian cosmos, so that the rites and offerings carried out within them would be magically effective on both the earthly and divine planes.

THE EGYPTIAN CONCEPT OF THE AFTERLIFE AND THE ROLE OF THE TOMB

The ancient Egyptians believed that the person was made up of six principal elements. The body, or *khet,* was the earthly abode in which the other elements resided during life. After death, if mummified properly, the *khet* was transformed into a *sah,* a divinized, perfected likeness of the deceased that could serve again as a receptacle for the intangible but essential parts of the person. During the funeral the *sah* was placed, ideally inside a nest of coffins and sarcophagi and surrounded by a variety of grave goods (see Chapter 7), in the burial chamber of the tomb. This would then be sealed and would house and protect the deceased for eternity.

The *ka* was the life-force, the eternal energy of the individual that survived after death and also formed a link to each person's ancestors and descendants. In images of royal births from the New Kingdom, the body and *ka* are shown being created together from clay by the potter god Khnum. Represented in art as outstretched

or upraised arms, it was the *ka* that was able to partake of the offerings made as part of the funeral and the mortuary cult. Perhaps closest in conception to the modern soul was the *ba*, also associated with the breath. According to the Pyramid Texts of the Old Kingdom, the *ba* left its owner at the moment of death and flew to the sky to dwell with the gods and the stars. Represented in art as a human-headed bird (see pp. 246–47), the *ba* could leave the tomb at night and roam the earth.

Another key element was the heart, or *ib*, which was seen as the seat of both intelligence and emotion. A person's name, *ren*, identified them, both during life and after death. The remembrance of the name was vital for directing the cult to the correct person, and an individual could be either helped or harmed magically through the invocation of his name. The shadow, *swt*, took the shape of the body, but lived on a different plane. It is generally shown as a black, featureless silhouette of the deceased, and is thought to have been able to emerge from the tomb during the day.

At the moment of death, the *ka* and *ba* left the body, and the deceased entered a dangerous period of limbo. The principal function of the funeral was to reunite the *ka* and *ba* with the body, and, through the performance of the proper rituals within the arena of the necropolis and tomb (see Chapter 5), to guarantee the perpetual rebirth of the deceased as a blessed spirit, or *akh*.

The Egyptian mythology of death seems to have been an amalgamation of several intertwined traditions. The earliest kings were thought to ascend after death to join the imperishable stars that circled the North Pole. By the middle of the Old

The tombs of the nobles at Thebes can be seen in part as miniature temples where the mortuary cult of the deceased was carried out. Ceremonies to perpetuate the memory of the tomb owner took place in the chapel, while during the major festivals honoring the departed the family of the deceased might gather for celebrations in a walled courtyard in front of the entrance, cut back into the cliff face (TT 97, the tomb of Amenemhet).

Kingdom, and certainly in the New Kingdom, kings, and by extension the elite who functioned as their delegates both in life and after death, were associated with the sun god, Re, and with the ruler of the Netherworld, Osiris.

In Egyptian mythology, Osiris was a member of the third generation of gods – son of the earth god Geb, and grandson of the creator god Atum. Primordial king of Egypt, Osiris was married to his sister, Isis. His jealous brother, Seth, murdered him, usurped his throne, and put his body into a chest and sent it out to sea. Isis managed to retrieve the chest after a long search, but Seth snatched the body once more and cut it into pieces, scattering them the length and breadth of Egypt. Isis and her sister Nephthys carefully collected all the pieces and reassembled Osiris's body, creating the first mummy. They were able to bring him back to life long enough for Isis to become pregnant with a son, Horus, before Osiris descended to the Netherworld, where he became king. Through his death and resurrection,

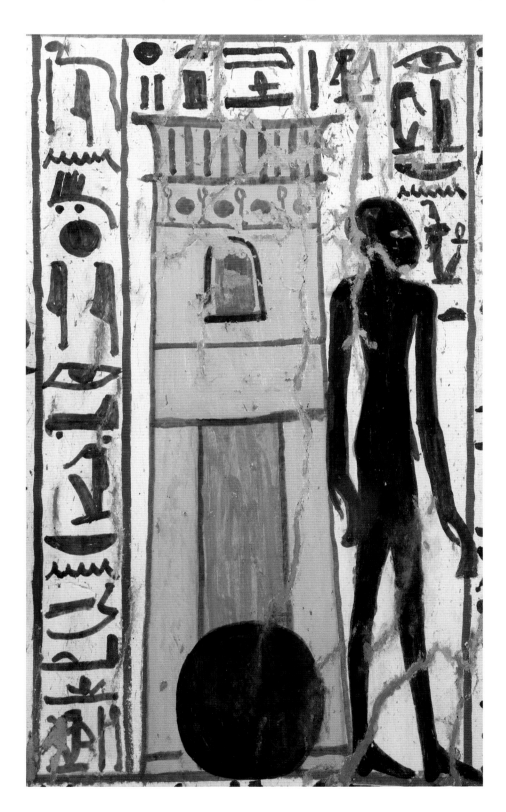

The shadow (*swt*) of the deceased emerges from the tomb in TT 219, the tomb of Nebenma'at (see also pp. 24–25). One of the six elements that made up the person according to Egyptian belief, the shadow was thought to be able to emerge from the tomb during the day.

The mortuary cult is celebrated for Roy (TT 255), Steward
in the Estates of Horemheb and Amun, with his wife,
Nebettawy, by a priest wearing a leopard-skin robe
accompanied by two mourning women. Roy holds
a lotus flower, a symbol of rebirth.

Osiris was connected with the fertility of the soil and the yearly cycle of the seasons. He was also linked with linear time, in which the universe had been created and would eventually come to an end.

Just as the sun set each night in the west and rose again each morning in the east, the sun god Re was imagined to die at dusk and descend to the Netherworld, through which he would travel in his night bark (*mesketet*) to join with Osiris in the deepest hours of the night. This joining with Osiris ensured the sun god's rebirth from the eastern horizon each morning as a child. The resurrected god traveled across the sky over the course of the daylight hours in his day bark (*mandjet*), aging during the afternoon and evening, to slip again beneath the western horizon as an old man. In this way Re was associated with a daily cycle of death and resurrection, and thus with cyclical time.

Within the underground part of the tomb the *sah*, the mummified and divinized body of the deceased, was associated with Osiris in the Netherworld, and, like the god, died and then joined with Re to be reborn as an *akh*. This transfiguration first took place during the embalming and at the funeral, where cult rituals and offerings transformed the mummy into a proper repository for the *ka* and *ba*. The mortuary cult was then carried out regularly within the tomb chapel to ensure that this resurrection was repeated and that the deceased was sustained in the afterlife. Ideally, this cult was carried out by the family of the deceased, led by the eldest son and heir, who took the role of Horus to the deceased's Osiris. According to the myth, as soon as he had reached his majority, Horus, as his father's rightful heir, challenged his evil uncle Seth for the throne of Egypt. After many battles, and trials before the gods, Horus defeated Seth and became king of Egypt. In a parallel and overlapping conception, Horus was also the son of Re.

The perpetual cult performed inside the tomb chapel, consisting of rituals and offerings of food and drink, would serve to reiterate the transfiguration and resurrection of the deceased, and provide for the magical sustenance of the *ka*. In reality, many private mortuary cults employed one or more professional priests to take the role of the eldest son and chief cult celebrant and were funded by endowments – gifts of estates – whose products were offered in the cult celebration, and then reverted to the use of the mortuary staff.

Most mortuary cults would have been performed on feast days, of which the Egyptian calendar contained a substantial list. The Theban necropolis would have been most active during the New Year's Festival and the Beautiful Feast of the Valley, both annual occasions when families were expected to visit the tombs of their relatives and honor their dead. During the Beautiful Feast of the Valley, the cult statue of Amun was brought out from its home in the inner chambers of Karnak Temple and, still hidden from public view inside a small shrine within a portable bark, it was then paraded to the river, and rowed across to the West Bank in a ceremonial barge. Once on the West Bank, it was taken to visit the memorial temple built for each deceased king before arriving at Deir el-Bahari, the place most sacred to Hathor, where first Mentuhotep II of the 11th Dynasty, then Hatshepsut, and finally Thutmose III had erected their own memorial temples.

Although the dead were no longer physically present in the earthly realm, they were believed still to be an integral part of the community, able to emerge from the tomb and appear to the living in dreams and visions. If they were not properly cared for they could cause illness and disaster, and the living could ask their deceased relatives (sometimes in the form of letters to the dead) to intervene in earthly affairs. By celebrating at the tomb, the family of the deceased entered a liminal zone, where the boundaries between the earthly and divine realms were blurred. The Beautiful Feast of the Valley in particular included several days of feasting and drinking, designed in part to create altered states of consciousness that could bring family members closer to their loved ones in the land of the Blessed Dead.

THE ARCHITECTURE OF THE ELITE TOMB
BEFORE THE NEW KINGDOM

The elite tombs of the New Kingdom developed from traditions firmly rooted in the preceding eras. The earliest Egyptian burials, from the Predynastic period, were merely holes in the ground into which the body was laid, most often curled into a fetal position; these graves were probably marked above by a simple mound of gravel or sand. However, for the elite, these basic tombs soon developed into much more elaborate complexes. By the Early Dynastic era, the wealthiest tombs included subterranean suites of chambers for the burial (some of which imitate the houses of the living, with bedrooms, magazines, servants' rooms, and even bathrooms), and mud-brick structures above, which often had niched walls in the fashion of contemporary dwellings. In earlier tombs this superstructure could be internally divided into chambers for additional storage; by the end of the 1st Dynasty it was a solid mass, and the burial goods were stored in the subterranean chambers. Niches in the eastern façade of the superstructure, often adorned with stelae with the name and image of the tomb owner, mark the place where the mortuary cult was celebrated. Some 1st Dynasty elite and royal burials were surrounded by subsidiary tombs, so that servants and courtiers could accompany their lords into the afterlife. I recently excavated several such tombs, around an elite *mastaba* at Saqqara. One was intact, and the body inside was covered with linen. Another tomb nearby dated to the 2nd Dynasty; the skeleton inside showed evidence of an early form of mummification.

Tombs with a built superstructure and excavated underground burial chambers continued to develop during the Old Kingdom. Instead of mud brick, however, stone began to be used for the superstructures; these tombs are known as

The *saff*-type tomb of Ametju (TT 83), Vizier under Thutmose III, at Sheikh Abd el-Qurna. The word *saff* comes from the Arabic for row, and this type of tomb had a line of pillars fronting the entrance to the chapel.

OPPOSITE ABOVE
The courtyard in front of TT 26 at Asasif, the tomb of Khnumemheb, a treasury official during the reign of Ramesses II; the tomb's entrance is flanked by two niches containing carved stelae (see p. 72).

OPPOSITE BELOW
This recently discovered tomb in the Asasif dates to the Ramesside period. The elegant hieroglyphs carved in sunk relief on the façade are prayers to help guarantee an eternal afterlife for the deceased.

A close-up of one of the stelae flanking the entrance to the tomb of Khnumemheb (TT 26), showing the deceased adoring Osiris, the ruler of the Netherworld, behind whom stands the Goddess of the West.

mastabas, after the Arabic benches they resemble. The fully niched wall style disappeared, but one or two niches were retained in the eastern façade to serve as the focus of the cult. These niches might be enclosed within an external wall, or cut deeper into the superstructure. The offering niche was gradually expanded into one or more chambers, forming a cult chapel. Where the landscape did not provide space for free-standing chapels, the entire complex could be cut into a cliff-face.

The First Intermediate Period, Middle Kingdom, and Second Intermediate Period were eras of great innovation, when a number of different tomb types appear for the first time. The *mastaba* form continued in use, especially in cemeteries of tombs of court officials clustered around the royal pyramids. One new type of tomb that appears in the Theban area during the First Intermediate Period is called by Egyptologists the *saff* tomb, after the Arabic word for "row." This consists of a large forecourt in the form of a T, with a pillared colonnade fronting the entrance to the chapel proper. In its simplest iteration, the chapel took the form of a long corridor leading back to the offering chambers. Another important Middle Kingdom type, also appearing at Thebes, was the inverse T-shape. Both of these tomb types were important for the development of the New Kingdom tomb at Thebes.

THE THEBAN TOMBS OF THE NEW KINGDOM
Like its predecessors, a typical New Kingdom tomb in its basic form had two principal levels – an upper cult chapel and a lower chamber or chambers for the burial itself. For most of the New Kingdom only the upper cult chapel was decorated, while the majority of burial chambers were left unadorned. Ideally, the tomb complex was

A view along a passage in the tomb of Kenamun (TT 93), Chief Steward of the King under Amenhotep II; at the far end is a niche containing a scene showing the deceased offering to Osiris and Anubis.

oriented east–west, though this was not always possible, and, if space allowed, was fronted by a walled courtyard terraced into the cliff-face, where the family of the deceased could gather during festival celebrations. Low rectangular platforms found in these courtyards are thought perhaps to have been used for the Opening of the Mouth ceremony (see p. 185). The façade of the tomb (which in the ideal tomb was the eastern wall) was smoothed, and sometimes decorated with rows of clay cones stamped with the name and titles of the tomb owner, along with the names of his wife or other members of his family. This façade, often adorned with sunk relief, was pierced by an entrance leading into the chapel where the cult was performed.

The most common form of the elite offering chapel in New Kingdom Thebes was an inverted T-shape, in which the chamber entered directly from the courtyard was generally wider than it was deep. In larger, more elaborate tombs, this transverse hall could be adorned with pillars left standing in the living rock when the rest was carved away. In its simplest form, the transverse hall was followed by a long corridor or passage that led to a niche or a small cult room. In the west wall of the corridor or the cult room were free-standing statues or rock-cut images of the deceased and members of his family. Either part or all of the chapel interior could be decorated with scenes and texts.

Shafts or sloping passages led from the floor of either the forecourt or the chapel down to burial suites for the tomb owner and his family. Many tombs were designed with two groups of subterranean apartments: one sloping passage led from the rear of the tomb to a burial chamber for the tomb owner and his wife, while a vertical shaft ending in a small chamber found in many tombs is thought to

The tomb chapel of Amenemhab (TT 85), an army commander whose career spanned the reigns of Thutmose III and Amenhotep II. The walls of the chapel have been plastered and covered with painted scenes, although these have suffered much damage.

have been a memorial dedicated either to the *ka* of the tomb owner or intended as a memorial for his parents. The mummy, in a nest of coffins, would be placed in the burial chamber at the end of the funeral, along with offerings of food and drink and other items that would be needed for the afterlife; the chamber was then sealed. It could be opened for the burial of another family member, but was otherwise inaccessible, and was meant to be closed for eternity.

A number of aspects of the tomb changed over time. In the 18th Dynasty, the courtyard was generally enclosed by round-topped walls built of stone or mud brick; after the Amarna period, the area in front of the tomb might be enclosed by higher walls, with the front wall in the form of a pylon (the monumental gateway to a temple), and a portico might be added. There could also be two courts instead of one. In general, the entire area fronting the chapel becomes more like a god's temple.

In earlier tombs, "autobiographies" – texts describing the lives and deeds of the tomb owners – were often carved on stelae flanking the entrance to the tomb. More common in the 19th and 20th Dynasties were hymns and other types of religious texts. Another major architectural difference between the earlier and later New Kingdom was the addition of a third level on top of the chapel, generally in the form of a pyramid and often including a figure of the tomb owner in a niche. This level was devoted specifically to the sun cult, whereas the interior of the tomb chapel was dedicated more to the cult of Osiris, king of the dead.

The repertoire of tomb shapes becomes greatly expanded from the reign of Amenhotep III on. Tombs grew larger and more complex, and more variations were possible. The repertoire of scenes changed as well, from images focused mainly on life on earth, the funeral itself, and the cult, to a greater emphasis on religious images and texts. In addition, the sloping passage leading to the main burial chamber might be more complex, for example with bends and turns, and the secondary tomb shaft moved from the interior of the chapel into the forecourt. Taken as a whole, the architecture of the Theban tombs shows both a great deal of continuity, but also an enormous amount of individual variety and innovation.

THE 18TH DYNASTY
The earliest elite tombs of the 18th Dynasty at Thebes, seen primarily at Dra Abu el-Naga, where the rulers of the 17th Dynasty had been buried, consisted of simple one-room chapels with burial shafts opening from their terraced forecourts. Lower-status tombs from later in the dynasty, such as that of Amenuserhat (TT 176), can also take this form.

The most common shape seen from the reigns of Thutmose I through Thutmose IV is the T-shape, with several basic variations. In some cases, these tombs were usurped from their Middle Kingdom owners. An early but typical example of this type is the tomb of Benia Pakhamun (TT 343), which has a forecourt, a transverse hall, and a long hall with a cult niche at the back. Access to the main burial chambers was generally through a shaft or a sloping passage from the back of the transverse hall. Good examples of the basic T-shape can be seen in the tombs of Menkheperreseneb (TT 86); Menkheper (TT 79); Djehutyemheb (TT 45); Userhat (TT 56); Djehutynefer (TT 80); Tjanuny (TT 74, unfinished); Amenhotep-si-se (TT 75); Hepu (TT 66); Menna (TT 69); Nebamun (TT 90); Neferrenpet (TT 249); and two anonymous tombs (TT 91 and TT 116). Useramun's chapel (TT 131) is in essence T-shaped, but the second hall is small and square rather than long, and its outer façade is adorned with a series of niches. These tombs belong to men with a wide range of titles, holding office in the state, palace, and temple administrations.

The tomb of Rekhmire (TT 100) is also a basic T-shape, but the long corridor is unique in that the height of ceiling gradually rises toward the ideal west (in fact the north), thus creating side walls that are trapezoidal rather than rectangular in shape and an extremely tall cult wall at the end. It is also unusual in that it includes no

The cult niche, where offerings would have been made to the deceased, in the tomb chapel of Neferrenpet (TT 249), who held the title Supplier of Dates/Cakes in the Temple of Amenhotep III during the mid-18th Dynasty.

burial chambers. It is likely that this valued official was awarded a burial suite in the Valley of the Kings, where there are several small tombs (comprised of substructure only, like all tombs in the Valley of the Kings) whose owners have never been identified.

Several early 18th Dynasty tombs combine the T-shape and the *saff* tomb. The tomb of Ineni (TT 81) is particularly interesting, as it takes an earlier *saff* tomb and converts it into a modified T-shape. In TT 71 Senenmut placed a row of pillars in his transverse hall which were then used to divide this chamber into individual sections, each with its own ceiling decoration. Like Rekhmire's tomb, TT 71 is anomalous in that it has no burial chambers below; Senenmut's burial suite (TT 353), consisting of a set of three stairways and passages leading to an antechamber and then a burial chamber, was shifted north so that it lies within the precinct of Hatshepsut's memorial temple at Deir el-Bahari. Other examples of the combined *saff* and T-shape are TT 83, the tomb of Ametju; TT 88 of Pekhsukher Tjenenu; TT 29 of Amenemopet Pairy; and, in smaller and more irregular form, TT 367 of Paser.

Some T-shaped chapels, especially from the reigns of Thutmose III and Amenhotep II, include extra chambers. One example from the reign of Thutmose III is the tomb of Puemre (TT 39); here, the long hall has been converted into a square chamber with a smaller cult chamber at the back, and two more chambers, both accessed from the transverse hall, have also been added. The subterranean chambers, which consist of a series of galleries at descending levels, are entered through a shaft at the north end of the transverse hall.

PAGES 77-78
The burial suite of the tomb of Senenmut, trusted advisor to the female pharaoh Hatshepsut (TT 353). The walls are covered with beautifully carved decoration, and above is a unique astronomical ceiling (see pp. 111-13). These subterranean chambers lie within the precinct of Hatshepsut's mortuary complex at Deir el-Bahari, while Senenmut's above-ground chapel is at Sheikh Abd el-Qurna.

PAGES 79-82
Three views of the main chamber in the tomb chapel of Amenemhat (TT 340), a royal artisan who lived during the 18th Dynasty: on the left is the north wall, with the deceased kneeling before Osiris and Anubis in the upper register, and a representation of the funeral below; in the center is a detail of the ceiling of TT 340, decorated to resemble a grape arbor; and on the right is the south wall, with the deceased again before Anubis and Osiris at the top, above two registers depicting a banquet at which the deceased and his wife are the recipients of the cult.

The tomb chapel of Nu and Nakhtmin (TT 291) – note the unfinished decoration on the wall visible to the left, with outlines drawn but none of the colors or details filled in. This is one of the few 18th Dynasty tombs at Deir el-Medina and has a two-chambered chapel.

PAGES 83–84
Detail of the ceiling of the tomb chapel of the royal artisans Nu and Nakhtmin (TT 291) at Deir el-Medina, decorated with rows of spirals and rosettes, and a band of text containing offering prayers.

The tomb of the army commander Amenemhab (TT 85) has an extra transverse hall, adorned with columns, added in front; Suenmut (TT 92) also has an extra pillared chamber before the transverse hall. A number of T-shaped chapels have square cult chambers added at the rear; these include the chapels of Amenemhat (TT 82); Duaneheh (TT 125); and Yamunedjeh (TT 84). The tombs of Senneferi (TT 99) and Horemheb (TT 78) have pillars in these additional cult chambers. Even more elaborate is the large tomb of Kenamun (TT 93), Chief Steward of Amenhotep II, which combines the T-shape and *saff* tomb, with a pillared cult chamber; this tomb is also one of the first to have an extensive substructure.

Also from the reign of Amenhotep II is the tomb of Sennefer (TT 96). This has a T-shaped chapel with the long hall leading to a pillared cult chamber with three cult niches in the west wall. Accessed through a stairway in one corner of the forecourt is a burial suite composed of an antechamber and pillared burial chamber. Sennefer's is one of the few decorated burial chambers from the 18th Dynasty.

The tombs of the high elite from the reign of Amenhotep III are anomalous, each having their own unique plan. In some cases, elements are taken from the basic T- and *saff* shapes, but these tombs also owe some of their design to contemporary "temple-tombs" at Saqqara, which are clearly modeled on the temples of the gods. Most of the Theban tombs from this reign that appear in this book are found on the lower slopes at Sheikh Abd el-Qurna, although the large tomb of Tiye's Chief Steward, Kheruef (TT 192), lies in the Asasif, and the tomb of Chief Sculptors Nebamun and Ipuky (TT 181) is at el-Khokha.

After the abandonment of Amarna early in the reign of Tutankhamun, a majority of late 18th Dynasty officials were buried at Saqqara rather than Thebes. Of those who built their tombs at Thebes, most return to the standard T-shape, with variations. These include the tombs of Amenhotep Huy (TT 40), with a pillared

Osiris, seated on a throne and with Anubis standing behind him, is offered incense and libations by Khonsu, High Priest of the cult of Thutmose III during the reign of Ramesses II. Khonsu's tomb (TT 31) at Sheikh Abd el-Qurna takes the form of a T-shape with a square cult chamber.

PAGE 88
A view toward the entrance stairway into the Ramesside burial suite of the royal artisan Amennakht (TT 218). On either side of the doorway, the deceased and his wife drink from pools of water; on the tympanum is the divine cow of the heavenly flood, Mehet-Weret.

PAGE 89
Looking toward the inner chamber of the tomb of Amennakht (TT 218), with Osiris seated before the Western Mountain. In the lower register, Amennakht and his sons Khaemteri (TT 220) and Nebenma'at (TT 219) raise their arms in adoration of the god.

offering chamber, Anen (TT 120), and Neferhotep (TT 50). The chapel of Roy (TT 255) is a single, roughly cut chamber with a cult niche at the back. Substructures during this era are generally accessed from the "south" side of the transverse hall.

The 18th Dynasty tombs at Deir el-Medina follow their own development, being for the most part simple chapels built of mud brick with burial suites carved into the rock below; in some cases additional chapels and burial suites have been added to the basic core. Few have survived from the 18th Dynasty; of the three examples seen here, two are simple one-room chapels (TT 340, Amenemhat, and TT 8, Kha), while the third, TT 291, for Nu and Nakhtmin, has a two-chambered chapel and shares a forecourt with the later tomb of Irunefer (TT 290).

THE 19TH AND 20TH DYNASTIES

Some of the chapels of the 19th Dynasty through the reign of Ramesses II are similar to their 18th Dynasty predecessors. A number are variant T-shapes, including those of Amenemopet (TT 177), which is a small, simple T-shape; Userhat (TT 51) and Neferhotep (TT 49), which are T-shaped with pillared cult chambers; and Khonsu (TT 31) and Nakhtamun (TT 341), which are T-shapes with square cult chambers. Burial suites, which grow more extensive but remain for the most part roughly carved and undecorated, now tend to be accessed from the forecourt, or from a side-wall in the innermost chamber. In some cases, these suites were sealed with only a wooden door, making multiple access for family burials easier. Several consist of two small chambers on a straight axis; examples of this type are the tombs of Neferrenpet (TT 178) and Piay (TT 263).

Considerably more elaborate is the tomb of Paser (TT 106), which has a forecourt with a niched façade, and pillars in both the transverse hall and the large second chamber. This tomb also illustrates the development of the substructure, which in the Ramesside era grows closer to the conception of the tomb as a model of the Netherworld, as seen in the royal tombs. From an entrance in the ideal south of the first hall, a series of four stairways trace the sides of a rectangle; a passage then leads to a pillared antechamber, from which four small storerooms are accessed, and finally ends in a small burial chamber.

Toward the end of the 19th Dynasty and through the 20th, the number of tombs of the high elite at Thebes continues to decrease, as resources dwindled and more officials moved their tombs north to the new capital in the Delta. The T-shape is still seen in the later Ramesside era, but these tombs tend to be smaller and belong to lower-status bureaucrats, for instance Amenemhab (TT 278) and Amenwahsu (TT 111). Imisibe (TT 65) usurped his T-shaped tomb with pillared transverse hall from an earlier official named Nebamun. The tombs of Shuroy (TT 13), Khonsumes (TT 30), Amoneminet (TT 277), and Nefersekheru (TT 296) have anomalous forms.

The most interesting corpus of tombs from the Ramesside era comes from Deir el-Medina. Of greatest interest here are the vaulted burial chambers; some of these were beautifully decorated, especially in the 19th Dynasty. The upper chapels were also decorated, but these have not survived nearly so well. Among them are the tombs of Sennedjem (TT 1); Pashedu (TT 3); Neferabet (TT 5); Amennakht and Nebenma'at (TT 218 and 219); Irunefer (TT 290); and Inerkhau (TT 359).

The next chapters will explore the decoration of the tombs within these architectural contexts. The specific religious concepts that lay behind each official's decision to place certain types of scenes in particular locations in his tomb is a fascinating area of scholarship that is only now beginning to be explored. Here we will review the content of the scenes themselves and the most common locations in which they are found, and discuss some of the basic principles believed to underlie these placement choices.

CHAPTER THREE

ART AND ARTISTS: THE DECORATION
OF THE THEBAN TOMBS

The architectural forms of the elite tombs at Thebes served as the frames for extensive scenes and texts. Most often, these covered only the walls of the cult chapels,
but sometimes also extended into the burial chambers. In the ancient Egyptian
conception, the elaborately drawn and painted scenes accompanied by hieroglyphic texts were more than purely decorative, they also had supernatural
properties: the depictions of the tomb owner, his family, and his world were imagined to be magically effective in the divine realm. For example, the representation
of an ideal funeral ensured that the burial rituals would be carried out perfectly in
the world beyond the grave. Images of the cult itself, including the performance of
rites and the presentation of offerings, guaranteed that the deceased would continue to be fed and cared for in the next world, even if the actual cult in the tomb
chapel ceased. Depictions of the tomb owner carrying out his official duties
memorialized his achievements and guaranteed both his eternal place in the Egyptian cosmos and the maintenance of the proper order of the cosmos itself.

The principal purposes served by these scenes were thus to ensure that the
deceased had a safe and successful rebirth and eternal existence in the next world,
and to celebrate and perpetuate the life that the tomb owner had lived on earth. Seen
in this light, it is perhaps easier for us to understand why the Egyptians dedicated so
much effort and expense in building, decorating, and furnishing their tombs.

The scenes and texts were arranged meticulously within their architectural
frames, and follow carefully designed progressions. It is thought that the Egyptians
had pattern books of sorts, from which tomb owners could choose the basic scene
types they wished to include. However, just as each chapel has its own architectural
form, the repertoire would have been deliberately and individually selected by its
owner in preparation for his eternal life, and the exact choice, execution, and placement of images are unique in each tomb. There is also a shift over time, from the
commemoration and idealization of the deceased's life on earth in the 18th
Dynasty, to an increased emphasis placed on the eternal afterlife in the divine realm
in the Ramesside era. Before addressing the content and meaning of the scenes
themselves, it is important to understand something of the technical processes, the
artists themselves, and the basic principles of Egyptian art.

TECHNIQUE AND PROCESS

The limestone strata that form the western cliffs at Thebes tend to be friable and are
not very suitable for the relief carving that was the preferred technique for Egyptian
monumental art. Although some chapels do include relief, most are decorated with
flat painting, allowing a great deal more freedom in the finer details. The tombs
were cut into the cliff using tools of flint and copper, then the rough, uneven surface
was entirely covered with a thick layer of mud plaster, made from vegetation-rich

(and probably foul-smelling) Nile silt mixed with chopped straw and sometimes stones. A thin layer of fine white plaster made from calcium sulphate (gypsum) applied on top provided a smooth surface for the application of the pigments.

The next step was to divide the walls into vertical sections and horizontal registers. This was done using a string dipped in red pigment that was held taut in a straight line and snapped against the wall. For large, formal figures at least, and in some cases for most of the wall, a standard grid of squares was laid down as a guide. Then, basing his work on a sketch drawn by the master artisan on a sheet of papyrus, a wooden board, or a flake of limestone known as an ostracon, an outline draftsman transferred the contours of the scene and text onto the wall in red pigment. With black or red ink, the master artisan would then make any necessary corrections to these lines. If the scene was to be in raised relief, the surface around the outlines was cut back and smoothed; if sunk relief (used mainly for exterior decoration) was desired, the figures themselves were cut back into the plaster. If the scene was to be painted, work could begin immediately.

Once the outlines were completed and corrected (although corrections could continue to be made at all stages), and, if required, the relief carved, the artists began to add color and interior detail. Pigments were mainly mineral-based, and used substances readily found in the Egyptian landscape. The first colors to be applied were black, made from a carbon derivative from a variety of sources, such as soot; creamy white, from limestone (calcium carbonate) or gypsum (calcium sulphate); bright white, from huntite (calcium carbonate mixed with magnesium); and red, from hematite (containing iron oxide). Other colors were then added:

OPPOSITE
Detail of a painted image of the cult celebrant, from the early 19th Dynasty tomb of the sculptor Ipuy (TT 217), showing the range of colors available to the ancient Egyptian artists.

BELOW
The drafted outlines of a figure of King Thutmose III, from the tomb chapel of Amenmesse (TT 89). The main contours of the desired design would be copied on to the wall in red ink following a sketch made by the master artist, who would then make any necessary corrections before the colors were applied and details filled in.

OPPOSITE
The grid used for controlling the proportions of the figures is still visible in the unfinished 18th Dynasty tomb of Suenmut (TT 92). The process of filling in the colors had begun, although here the figures seem to have been left until last.

BELOW
Note the modeling and surface detail of this baboon-headed deity (one of the Four Sons of Horus) from the late 18th Dynasty tomb of Nebamun and Ipuky (TT 181), rendered entirely with pigment. (For the whole of this scene, see p. 201.)

yellows and browns came from ochers (clay containing iron oxides); green came from wollastonite, with a high copper content, or malachite (copper carbonate); and blue was made by mixing and heating together three substances (a calcium compound, a copper compound such as malachite, and a silicate such as quartz) in the correct proportions, resulting in a vitreous substance known as frit. Different shades of blue and green were made by grinding this frit to varying degrees of fineness. Green could also be made by mixing blue with yellow. Exceptionally, gold might be used for special details. Varying shades of the pigments could be created by mixing them with white or black; otherwise, colors were rarely mixed.

To bind them to the plaster, the pigments were combined with a type of plant gum; for the frits, an animal glue may also have been used. The colors were applied to the walls using brushes of various sizes made from reeds and fiber; like modern artists, the ancient Egyptians used a range of brushes depending on the level of detail desired. It is interesting to note that blue and green, the colors for which frits were used, had to be applied much more thickly, with additional binder. These have therefore been the first colors to fall off the walls, often leaving behind pale ghosts of their original hues.

The best examples of New Kingdom Theban painting exhibit a great deal of creativity in the details. Textures were rendered by careful use of brushwork. Delicate painting can be seen in small features, such as the folds of a dress, the fur of an animal, or the feathers of a bird. Diaphanous costumes were painted directly on top of the still damp skin color with bright white, then immediately brushed partly off. Other layering techniques were also used to excellent effect. Wax could also be used to create textures and effects.

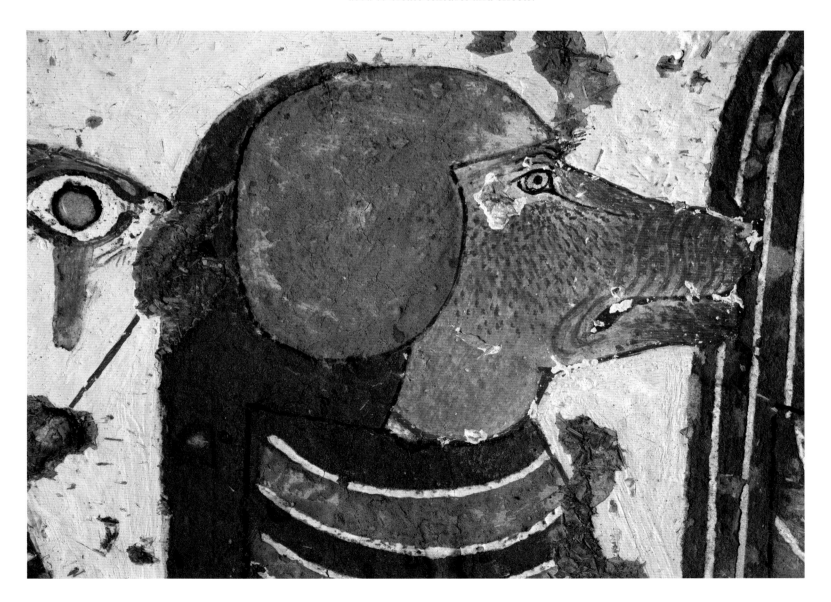

THE ARTISTS

Who were the artists who decorated the private tombs of Thebes? The carvings and paintings found in the nobles' tombs are often of outstanding quality, and show enormous skill. There must certainly have been a number of master artists designing and supervising the execution of the decoration of the tombs, and some Egyptologists are beginning to be able to identify the hands of individuals. Based on detailed analysis, one scholar believes that the chapels of Menna (TT 69), Nakht (TT 52), Nebseny (TT 401), and the tomb of Amenhotep III were the work of a single artistic genius. Another scholar attributes the tombs of Menna, Nakht, and Nebamun, all of which have been dated to the end of the reign of Amenhotep III, or perhaps the beginning of the reign of Akhenaten, to a single artist or group of artists.

It is important to remember that in ancient Egypt art was not for the sake of art. It was for the sake of religion. This is why we do not have the names of most Egyptian artists: their work was for the glory of the gods, not for their own aggrandizement. However, the names of several artists have been preserved. From the Old Kingdom, we have Iri Tetiseneb, who tells us in his tomb at Saqqara that he carried out the work with his own hands. Seni from Akhmim, in Middle Egypt, informs us that he decorated the tombs of his father and son. The artists employed in the tomb of Kai that I discovered at Giza are acknowledged in an unusual inscription: "it is the tomb makers, the draftsmen, the craftsmen, and the sculptors who made my tomb. I paid them beer and bread and made them satisfied." From Thebes, the artist Amunweserhat is named in the tomb of Amenhotep-si-se (TT 75) and the artist Amunbarnnefer is seen the tomb of Nebamun and Ipuky (TT 181).

ABOVE
Much of Egyptian art is very ordered and organized into registers, but the artists were also capable of creating compositions of great life and freedom. Here a panel in the tomb of Khonsu (TT 31) teems with birds and insects.

PAGES 97–98
The High Priest of the Royal *Ka* of Thutmose I, Userhat, is shown receiving offerings in the painted decoration from his early 19th Dynasty tomb chapel (TT 51). The rough mud plaster used to prepare the wall surface is visible beneath the surface.

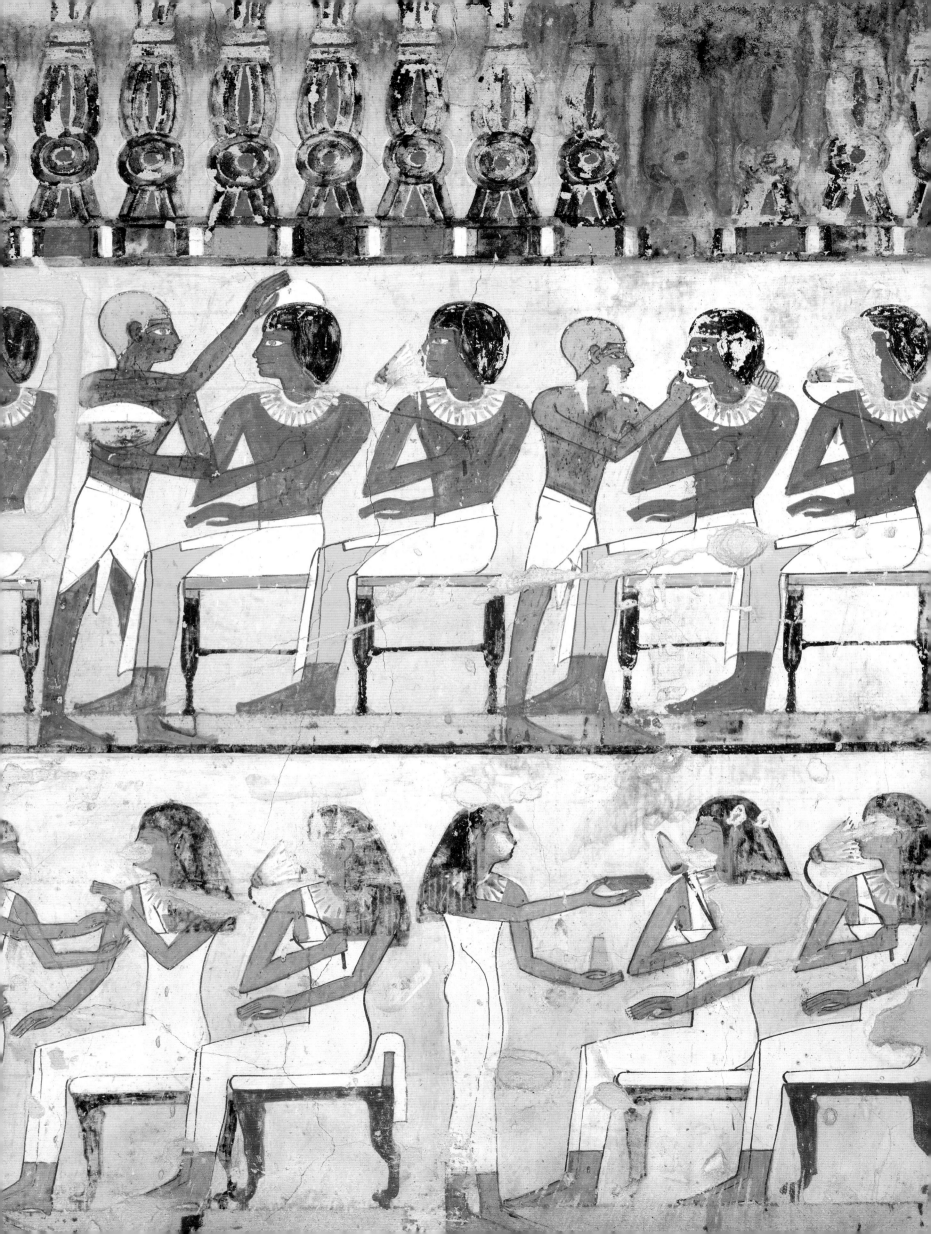

This image of the royal artisan Irunefer (TT 290) drinking from a pool of water shaded by a palm tree demonstrates the Egyptian concept of "perspective," which was intended to convey information rather than mirror reality exactly.

PAGES 99–100
A banqueting scene from the tomb of Suenmut (TT 92) demonstrates the ability of the ancient Egyptian artists to use precise shades effectively. The colors of the skin tones of the men and women and servants are clearly differentiated.

We do know a good deal about the community of artisans who lived at Deir el-Medina and who built and adorned the royal tombs in the Valley of the Kings. It is likely that they were also hired or lent out for some of the private tombs. A newly discovered tomb at Saqqara, dating to the reigns of Amenhotep III and Akhenaten, was built for Thutmose and Qenamun, who the excavator believes may have been involved in the decoration of a number of Theban tombs, including that of Nebamun (TT 90). These two were royal artisans bearing the title "Overseers of Draftsmen in the Place of Truth," who were thus responsible for tombs in the Valley of the Kings. We also have the names of some of the workmen and artists connected with the Temple of Karnak, especially in the 19th Dynasty. From their titles, we learn that some of these artisans also worked at Luxor Temple and in the royal memorial temples on the West Bank. Perhaps artists from the workshops connected to the Amun and royal temples were also responsible for some of the work on the private tombs, but we do not really know for sure.

From the discovery of paintings in which the hands of masters and students can be traced, it seems that the training of artists in ancient Egypt was based primarily on copying and repetition. Individual students were probably assigned to a master, who would teach them the principles of art and set them to copying drawings. Once they had reached a certain level, apprentices were permitted to execute painting in the tombs, beginning probably with the simple application of color and advancing to painting interior details, before moving on to sketching minor figures. Eventually, the student would become the master, and the cycle would continue.

According to the conventions of Egyptian art, the human figure was typically represented in a combination of frontal and profile view, as seen here in the seated figures in the tomb of Khonsumes (TT 30). The legs and lower torso are in profile, as are the arms, while the shoulders and visible eye are shown from the front.

PRINCIPLES OF EGYPTIAN ART

When looking at the scenes in Egyptian monuments, it is important to understand the basics of pharaonic art. Traditional Western art, which has grown out of the Classical tradition, sets out to reproduce reality as accurately as possible. Conventions such as perspective, based around a vanishing point, and the point of view of the artist, are key to this practice. Images of specific people are often portraits, capturing the physiognomy of the subject as exactly as possible. Landscapes and interiors are designed as echoes of nature and real architecture.

By contrast, the primary purpose of Egyptian art was to convey information. Take, for example, the typical representation of the human figure: the legs and lower torso are shown in full profile, the upper torso is shown twisted so that it is partly profile and partly frontal, the arms are in profile, and the face is in profile, except that the visible eye is shown as if from the front. Boxes are often depicted with their key contents, which in reality would have been concealed inside, as if they were on top of them, so that the viewer knows what they contained. Furniture is also shown in a combination of profile and frontal views.

Most Egyptian monumental art is fairly regimented. Walls are generally divided into vertical sections, and the sections in turn into horizontal registers. Within each register, the figures are arranged almost geometrically, at regular intervals.

OPPOSITE
Lines of offering bearers from the tomb of the army commander Amenemhab (TT 85) illustrate both the use of registers to organize scene complexes and the desire to convey information – in this case the objects carried by each person – as clearly as possible (for more of this scene, see pp. 136–37).

OVERLEAF
These marsh plants and birds from the tomb of the Scribe of Recruits Horemheb (TT 78) are carefully organized, yet give an impression of freedom.

Files of servants depicted bringing offerings to the tomb owner, for example, are all of the same size and shape, and walk in the same direction with the same stride – any differences between them consist of the details of what they are wearing and carrying; cattle, shown being herded across a canal, will be identical, their bodies overlapping and only the colors and patterns on their hides distinguishing one from the other. Architecture is rarely depicted, but when it is, structures are represented in the form of elaborate hieroglyphs.

However, there is a significant amount of freedom in the painting of the Theban tombs, especially in the details. For example, figures placed in rows can have individual costumes and hairstyles, and some variation in their poses. The style of the art is also dependent to some degree on the type of scene in question. Formal images of the tomb owner seated before an offering table, or of the king in his kiosk, tend to be relatively rigid and static. Standard scenes of such activities as agriculture and manufacture often have an overall formality, but can be filled with wonderful, free details. In general, images of the tomb owner and his family are usually the most formalized, while depictions of servants and peasants may be much freer.

Scenes that portray the chaotic world at the fringes of the Egyptian cosmos, which surrounded and continually threatened it, are the freest of all. Icons of the tomb owner hunting and fishing in the marshes (see below, p. 154) are filled with clumps of papyrus teeming with birds and animals, and waterways in which fish of a variety of species swim. In desert hunts, the register lines are often dispensed with, so that the animals are scattered across the landscape. Yet even within these freer types, the Egyptian love of order and harmony is evident: in hunting and

OPPOSITE
A free and lively rendering of a sycomore fig tree (*Ficus sycomorus*), with two small birds perched on its branches, from the early 19th Dynasty tomb of Userhat (TT 51).

All of these offering bearers from the tomb of Amenemhat (TT 82) are identical in size and basic posture, but they differ in various details of their gestures and the objects they are carrying, creating a vivid and interesting scene.

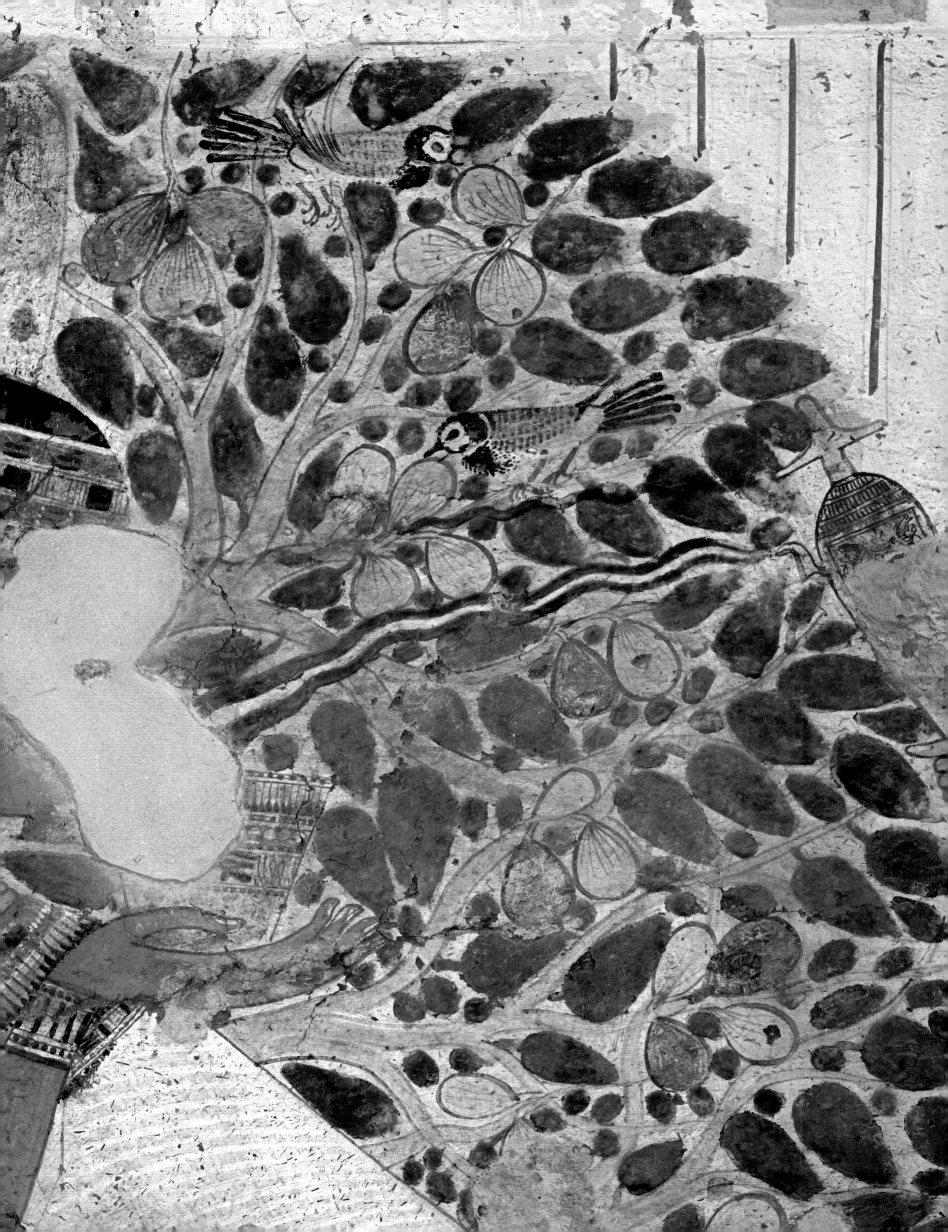

fishing scenes, mirror images of the tomb owner are arranged facing one another, with the elements of one scene balancing the corresponding elements in the other.

THE SCHEME OF DECORATION

In the 18th Dynasty, it seems the aim was to decorate as much as possible of the tomb chapel, while the burial chamber was rarely decorated; in Ramesside times, however, and most particularly at Deir el-Medina, this desire could be extended to the burial chamber as well. This ambition was not, of course, always fulfilled: many tombs were only partly finished when the tomb owner died and was buried, leaving the remainder of the tomb unadorned. It would seem there was a hierarchy of importance in terms of the areas decorated first, and those left for last. It was important to carve at least the name and titles of the owner on the outer doorway, and it was crucial that the cult niche at the back be equipped with some sort of cult focus so that the deceased could receive the offerings made there. Next the transverse hall, as the first area seen by visitors to the tomb, had precedence, with the two walls facing the doorway into the tomb and flanking the entrance to the long hall being the most important in this room. These two walls are considered by scholars to be the focal points for visitors, and so key scenes would be placed here.

Many ceilings were painted with geometric patterns that give the effect of textiles, as if the chapel (or burial chamber) was a fabric tent. Perhaps the most unusual and creative ceiling is to be found in the burial chamber of Sennefer (TT 96B). Here, the rock was left uneven and painted with bunches of grapes, making the visitor feel as if the chamber were a grape arbor.

On most walls, there was a dado around the bottom part, which was usually left undecorated for the majority of its height. Above this, the decoration generally extended to occupy most of the height of the walls. At the top, the scenes were bordered by the traditional *khekher* frieze, imitating bundles of reeds tied together, framed above and at the sides by rows of colored rectangles. Within this frame, the scenes were arranged inside vertical boxes, usually further divided into horizontal registers. In the 18th Dynasty, there is a tendency to use each wall, or vertical section of wall, for a single subject or scene complex. Later, the decorated surfaces are often divided into horizontal strips, with the lower band illustrating the mortuary cult and the upper band depicting the realm of the gods.

It is not always easy to assign individual scenes found in the Theban tombs to clear-cut categories, but they can be divided roughly into those that illustrate life on earth, reflecting the activities carried out by the tomb owner while alive – his "first life" – and those connected directly to the funeral and the afterlife, including vignettes from various Netherworld books. A third category consists of images related to the cult meal, including icons of the tomb owner and his family at tables piled high with offerings, and images of the funerary and ongoing cults being performed. These are the core of the tomb's decoration – the most essential type of scene. A significant subcategory of this type consists of the false doors and statues that form important cult foci in the tomb chapels. In addition to depictions of the cult meal, this third category includes banqueting scenes, which are both an extension of the cult celebration and an image of the ideal feast on earth.

Over the course of the New Kingdom, there is a shift away from scenes commemorating the life of the tomb owner on earth toward icons illustrating the afterlife in the divine realm. In general, especially during the 18th Dynasty, the "earthly life" scenes tend to be in the transverse hall, while funerary and religious scenes are found in the long halls and in the burial chambers. Banqueting and cult scenes appear in a number of places in the tomb. Rock-cut cult statues, cult chambers, and cult niches are always at the far end of the tomb chapel, in the ideal west. Decoration in burial chambers, when it is found, is almost always concerned with life after death.

PAGES 109–10
The ceilings in tombs were often painted with geometric patterns that resemble textiles, but here in the tomb of Sennefer (TT 96) the uneven surface of the rock was painted with trailing vines and bunches of grapes, creating the illusion of a grape-covered arbor.

PAGES 111–13
The burial chamber of Senenmut (TT 353) is adorned by a unique, unfinished astronomical ceiling; this type of ceiling is generally seen only in royal contexts from later periods. The skill of the master artist at work is evident in the rendering of the figures.

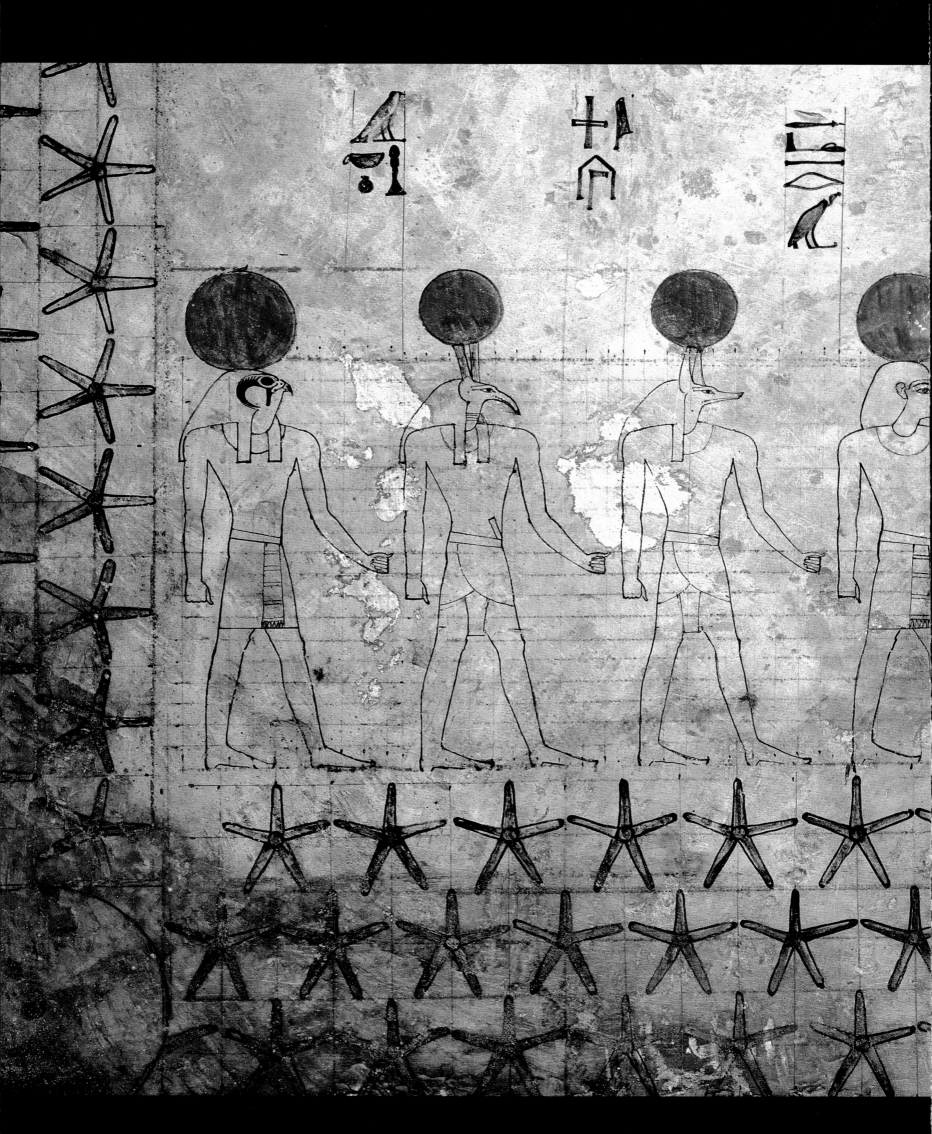

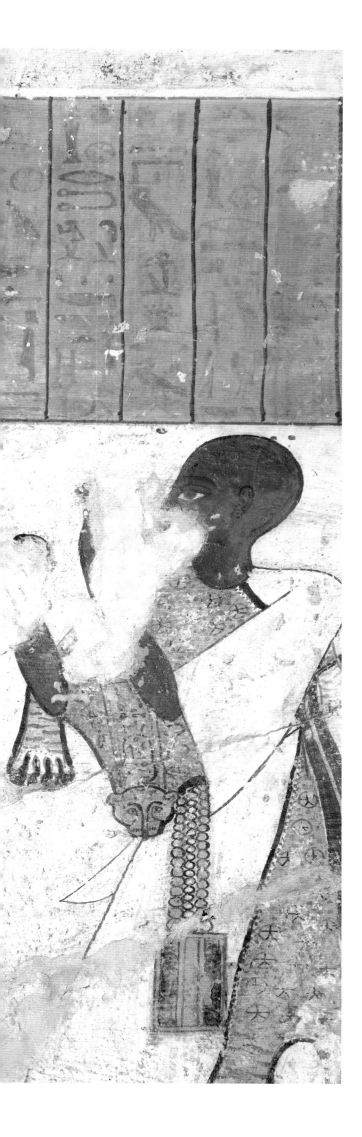

The vizier Usermontu offers incense to the bark of Montu as part of his official duties during the festival held in honor of that god, in a scene from the tomb of his brother, the High Priest of Thutmose III, Khonsu (TT 31).

CHAPTER FOUR
SCENES OF EARTHLY LIFE

The richest corpus of scenes in the Theban tombs, especially those of the 18th Dynasty, falls under the heading of life on earth. At the core of this category are scenes generally thought to be representations of important events in the tomb owner's actual career, or in the ideal career that he would have hoped for during life and wished to continue after death. Such "earthly life" scenes include images of the high official accompanying the pharaoh on important religious occasions; presiding over the ceremonies at which the king received foreign tribute; supervising agricultural or other activities relating to the production of food; overseeing the manufacture of a variety of items, from bows and arrows, to jewelry, to colossal statues; and supervising the delivery of goods from the Egyptian provinces. Other images included in this category depict the tomb owner fishing and fowling in the marshes or hunting in the desert.

These scenes can be interpreted on a number of levels, from the literal to the highly symbolic. On the most straightforward level, the images offer us a glimpse into an idealized life on earth for the tomb owner, his family, and dependants. We can see, for example, the entire agricultural cycle, from preparing the fields to harvesting the produce, and can even study the equipment that the ancient Egyptian farmers used. Manufacturing scenes inform us about tools, techniques, and the products of a variety of workshops. From tribute scenes, we learn about the costumes and luxury goods of Egypt's neighbors. Overall, we are provided with information about the administrative and bureaucratic organization of the court.

At the same time, these scenes and texts were also intended to serve as symbols that commemorated the deceased's actions on the earthly plane and perpetuated his or her eternal memory and identity, providing a magical model for their next lives in the Fields of the Blessed. On yet another level, iconic images such as dominion over foreigners or the spearing of fish or the hunting of desert animals were designed magically to subdue the chaotic elements that surrounded and continually threatened the Egyptian cosmos.

Scenes of earthly life are significantly more common during the 18th Dynasty, and decrease in number during the Ramesside era. They tend to be placed in the outer, or transverse, hall of the T-shaped chapel, but could continue into the chamber beyond. Placement of individual scene types is not particularly consistent from one tomb to the next, but some general patterns can be recognized. In many T-shaped chapels, especially of the 18th Dynasty, the most important scenes were placed on the west wall of the transverse hall, flanking the entrance to the interior room or rooms. Scholars have identified these scenes as focal points of the decoration, placed where they would be the first and most prominent images seen by visitors to the chapel. Of the "earthly life" scenes, those most often found in this important position are images of either the king himself, shown seated on a throne

Amenhotep III, with his Great Royal Wife, Tiye, standing behind him, receives offerings from the priest Ameneminet (not visible) in the transverse hall of Ameneminet's tomb (TT 277). The king holds the crook and flail in one hand and an *ankh* in the other. Scenes involving the king were often placed where they would be most prominent and immediately visible to visitors to the tomb.

within a kiosk or shrine and receiving gifts from the tomb owner; or of a god receiving offerings; or of the tomb owner.

THE KING IN A KIOSK

The pharaoh stood at the center of the Egyptian cosmos. As the intermediary between his subjects and the world of the gods, and of divine blood himself, he was the fount from which all things flowed. As the ultimate earthly authority, the king – in theory at least – appointed all officials and priests, and every member of the elite thus owed his or her position and wealth directly to the monarch. The importance of the king to the members of his court and administration is reflected by his appearance in their tombs.

The icon of the king seated within a kiosk is first found in the reign of Hatshepsut, and is most popular through the reign of Thutmose IV. Although each example of this type of image is different in its details, the king is always shown facing out, with his back to the ideal east–west axis of the tomb. He sits on a throne within a platform that is decorated most often with images of vanquished enemies of Egypt or friezes of hieroglyphs representing life, stability, and dominion. Some platforms are preceded by a ramp or stairs, echoing a hieroglyph for *ma'at*, the proper order of the universe (also personified by the goddess Ma'at), and thus the king is metaphorically upheld by this concept. Other details of the kiosk are also full of symbolism: the throne on which the king sits is often formed of two lions, representing the animals who guarded the horizons and thus the entrances to the day (earthly) and night (Netherworld) skies; the king can be seen in this context as an incarnation of the sun god, rising and setting in the daily solar cycle of death and rebirth. The *uraei* (cobras) crowned with solar disks that often top the kiosk also have close links to the sun.

The king himself appears in a variety of costumes, and the surviving scenes provide us with a partial litany of pharaonic crowns, including the blue "war helmet," the *nemes* headcloth, and the elaborate *shuty* crown made up of ostrich feathers, cow's and ram's horns, and a sun disk, all worn over a wig tied with a fillet. Each of these crowns had its own symbolism: for example, the *shuty* crown with the fillet identified the king with Horus, and is generally seen in contexts related with the New Year's Festival, while the *nemes* headdress was linked with the sun god, Re. The king typically holds his crook and flail, instruments respectively of rule and protection. He might also hold an *ankh*, symbolizing life, a mace with which to smite Egypt's enemies, or a variety of staffs.

The entire kiosk is set beneath the sign that represents the vault of the sky, a long rectangle with a lower edge that curves down at each end. The background of the scene is traditionally golden, the color of divinity, which can also be interpreted as reflecting the light of the sun on the earthly plane. Accompanying the king might be a member of the royal family (most often the queen), a god or goddess, or an image of the royal *ka*, the king's double or life-force.

Scholars believe that this kiosk represents an actual small canopied dais that would have been set up in the audience hall of the royal palace, where the king would sit to hear petitions and meet with courtiers, nobles, and ambassadors from far-off lands. Associated with this image are extensive scenes depicting various activities in which the tomb owner was involved, such as the supervision of foreign tribute or the provisioning of troops; in many cases these cover most of the remainder of the west walls of the transverse hall.

Outside the kiosk itself, but still closely related to it, is often the tomb owner himself, sometimes standing facing the pharaoh and offering him gifts. Such a gift might consist of a bouquet made up of papyrus, poppy, and lotus – plants which together connote creation, fertility, protection, and eternal life. Several tomb owners attend to the king by fanning him or raising their arms in gestures of adoration. In

Beneath the elaborate throne of Queen Tiye, a cat embraces a pintail duck while a monkey jumps over them, in a royal kiosk scene from the tomb of the Second Priest of Amun, Anen (TT 120).

other cases, the tomb owner offers a gift that is related directly to the scene covering the rest of the same wall, such as grown or manufactured items. One example (TT 76) shows the tomb owner supervising the creation and presentation of gifts for the New Year's Festival; another, from the tomb of the Second Priest of Amun under Thutmose IV, Amenhotep-si-se (TT 75), depicts the deceased supervising the manufacture of gifts to be offered by the king to the Temple of Amun-Re at Karnak. The inscription associated with the scene provides a clear description of Amenhotep-si-se's role: "Supervising monuments and placing them in the Presence [i.e. the presence of the king] in order to view [each of] the works as was commanded, that which his Majesty desired doing [what] satisfies the heart of … Amun … and seeking to do what is good for his temple, and adorning his temple with electrum." It is fascinating to note that the gifts represented in the tomb of Amenhotep-si-se are echoed in reliefs carved in his monarch's Peristyle Court at Karnak, and even, in one case, by an actual statue that is now in the Egyptian Museum, Cairo.

OTHER ROYAL IMAGES

With the shift in emphasis from scenes of "earthly life" to those relating to afterlife and cult activities in the Ramesside era, images of the living king are much less frequent. In later tombs, the king might also be seen in the company of the gods. Divinized kings are also more common in the late 18th through 20th Dynasties, or in the context of the Beautiful Feast of the Valley (see pp. 135 and 229).

Several of the Theban tombs contain unusual images of the king, generally related in some way to the titles of the tomb owner. There are, for example, images of a king as a child seated on the lap of his tutor or nurse or being suckled by his wet nurse, for instance in TT 85, the tomb of Amenemhab, commander of soldiers. Several tombs, including that of Khaemhat Mahu (TT 57), depict the king being suckled by a goddess. Two scenes from the mid-18th Dynasty show the king hunting (in TT 143, an anonymous tomb at Dra Abu el-Naga, and TT 72, belonging to a priest named Re). The king can also be seen in the context of a festival, as in the tomb of Kheruef (TT 192), where Amenhotep III appears (along with his Great Royal Wife, Tiye) in a number of scenes connected with his Sed Festival (see p. 137).

SCENES OF FOREIGN TRIBUTE

Extensive scenes representing the presentation of foreign tribute to the monarch are found in a number of high-status tombs of the 18th Dynasty, most often belonging to viziers. In these instances, it is the tomb owner himself who appears to be responsible for the organization and proper implementation of the ceremonies involved. Most tribute scenes include chieftains or princes from a number of different lands, with each entourage arranged in one or more registers. Each group is distinguished from the others by carefully chosen skin colors, physical features, and costumes, and by the objects they carry.

It should be noted that, although they are usually referred to as "tribute" scenes, the mechanism by which the luxury goods were delivered to Egypt is not always clear, and it is possible that different countries had different relationships with the pharaoh. Some vassal states or conquered lands might have owed true tribute, for which Egypt offered nothing in return. Other foreign princes shown bringing gifts might have been hoping to win pharaonic favor, while in other cases a straightforward exchange of trade goods might be implied. In fact, some scholars doubt whether the Egyptians had direct contact with all of the various types of

The army commander Amenemhab was awarded a large tomb in the Valley of the Nobles (TT 85), most probably on the merits of his wife, Baky, who bore the title Chief Royal Nurse. In this scene from the New Year's Festival, Baky is shown suckling a prince, while her husband offers her a bouquet of Amun.

Groups of courtiers and foreign envoys from Nubia, Libya, and the Syro-Palestinian area – each with distinctive costume and hairstyles – bow and offer homage in this sketch of a tribute scene from the tomb of the vizier Ramose (TT 55). Scenes such as this one, and that from the tomb of Rekhmire (pp. 127–30), provide us with unparalleled information about the countries that Egypt had dealings with during the New Kingdom.

foreigners represented. Whatever the full story behind these images, they are certainly fascinating, and provide a wealth of detail about the costumes and luxury goods of Egypt's neighbors.

An excellent example of such a tribute scene is found on the left focal wall in the transverse hall of Rekhmire's tomb chapel (TT 100; pp. 127–30). It includes all the main groups of foreigners depicted in most such scenes and opens a wonderful window into the cosmopolitan world of New Kingdom Egypt. In the top register are people from the Land of Punt, a civilization which has left little trace on the ground but is believed to have been located somewhere in the vicinity of modern Eritrea or Sudan. Famed for its incense trees, Punt was the goal of some of Egypt's most ambitious trade expeditions, including a famous one sent by Hatshepsut. The typical Puntite costume was a divided kilt, while hairstyles changed over time. The men of the Puntite delegation bring incense trees in baskets, as well as baboons, ibex, monkeys, and cheetahs. In the next registers are the "Keftiu," their fringed kilts, boots, hairstyles, and the goods they bring clearly identifying them as Aegean, although their exact origin within the "Middle Sea" is still under debate. In their hands they bear precious vessels in the Aegean style, such as rhyta (ritual vessels for liquids) topped with the heads of bulls, ibex, and lions.

In the third register, Nubians from Kush lead exotic animals such as giraffes, baboons, monkeys, and leopards. Other luxury gifts borne by these chieftains and their entourages from the far south are ivory, ostrich eggs, and rings of gold from the desert mines. The foreigners of the fourth register, with long hairstyles and calf-length fringed robes, are labeled Chiefs of Retjenu, the ancient name for the Syrian region. Like the Nubians, they come with animals, in this case horses, an elephant, and a bear; they also offer weapons and vessels most likely filled with precious substances. The fifth register may represent a group of prisoners, as both Nubian and Syrian men, women, and children are shown, along with a military escort. Perhaps these were brought by the other groups in order to demonstrate their loyalty to pharaoh; in fact, some children of Egypt's vassals and allies are known to have been raised at the Egyptian court. Each of the foreign delegations pile their offerings in front of Egyptian scribes, who record every item in detail, all supervised by Rekhmire himself as the king's deputy.

OPPOSITE
Foreign envoys, identifiable by their dress and the objects they carry, lead in small children by the hand, in this tribute scene from the tomb of the High Priest of Amun, Menkheperreseneb (TT 86); the children would then be brought up and educated at the Egyptian court.

In addition to their historical importance and the rich information they provide about foreign relations in the New Kingdom, tribute scenes also served a symbolic purpose. Foreigners were the earthly embodiments of the forces of chaos that constantly surrounded and threatened the created world. It was therefore an essential task of the king to vanquish Egypt's enemies and thus protect the cosmic order. In royal monuments, this concept was expressed by scenes showing the pharaoh smiting foreign princes and winning great battles over enemies. Here, in the private realm, the maintenance of order over chaos is evoked by scenes such as these, in which foreign princes and chieftains are eternally shown in postures of obedience and submission, bringing the best of their native lands to enrich the coffers of the pharaoh.

PROVISIONING OF TROOPS

Of the numerous tombs belonging to military officials, several depict ceremonies related to the recruiting, registration, and provisioning of soldiers or conscripts. Each of these representations differs slightly in its general organization and details, but all are closely linked to the king in his kiosk, both through their location on the tomb wall and by the gifts presented by the tomb owner to his monarch. In such scene complexes, the tomb owner generally appears numerous times, supervising the various activities that are being carried out, and then turning to offer the fruits of his labors to his king, while rows of recruits wait to be registered before they receive their training.

OPPOSITE AND BELOW
In these two scenes from the tomb of the Commander of Soldiers under Thutmose IV, Tjanuny (TT 74), a herd of cattle and a file of recruits are brought toward a figure of the tomb owner (not visible here). A scribe, holding a stylus and his palette with ink well, records the recruits as they come before him.

PAGES 124–26
A line of the anthropomorphized names of several of Egypt's traditional enemies of different nationalities are shown with their arms tied behind their backs, in an image of eternal defeat; a detail from the base of a throne of Amenhotep III painted in the tomb of the Chief Steward of Tiye, Kheruef (TT 192).

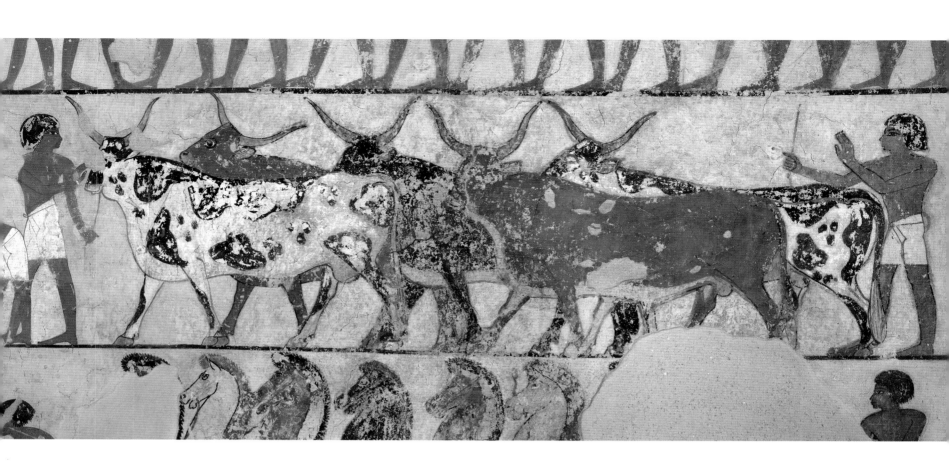

PAGES 127–30
Two registers from the great tribute scene in the tomb of Rekhmire (TT 100). Above, Nubians bring gold, skins, and ivory, and lead in exotic animals, all easily identifiable; below, Syrians carry vessels made of precious metals, pottery jars most likely filled with oil or wine, metal ingots, a chariot, as wells as horses and a bear. Before the envoys are piles of goods already offered to pharaoh. As Vizier, Rekhmire would have officiated over such ceremonies.

PAGES 131–32
A group of new recruits chat with one another or sit disconsolate and homesick, while one has his hair cut, in the tomb of the Royal Scribe Userhat (TT 56).

Certain details in the Theban scenes suggest that military service was not necessarily voluntary. In the tomb of Horemheb (TT 78) the men in one group of recruits have their arms tied behind their backs, indicating that the ancient Egyptians did use mass conscription to assemble the manpower needed to fight in the army and carry out civil projects such as construction and quarrying. Such practices date back at least to the Old Kingdom, when the pyramid, the pharaoh's monumental tomb, was Egypt's national project. Then, as in the New Kingdom, loyal Egyptians from all over the country would send their young men to serve the monarch, offering their labor, along with grain and other foodstuffs, in lieu of taxes.

It is interesting to note that not all recruits are native Egyptians; foreigners could also join pharaoh's army, and prisoners of war could earn their freedom through such service. Syrians and other foreign princes are shown in some tombs as higher-ranking envoys, evidently there to observe. Many fascinating details can be found in these scenes, which are filled with a variety of figures, including priests, soldiers, oxen, and horses, in addition to the recruits themselves, making the walls lively and interesting. After being conscripted, the troops of soldiers and workers would have been outfitted, assigned to their various divisions, and required to pledge allegiance to pharaoh, before receiving their training. Texts suggest that ancient "boot camp" consisted of a combination of discipline and corporal punishment.

HONORS AND AWARDS

Also related to the Royal Kiosk icon are a number of scenes that depict the tomb owner being honored with gifts or installed in a new office, both actions that flowed directly from the pharaoh. Such scenes are most often seen at Thebes in the reigns of Amenhotep III and his son, Amenhotep IV/Akhenaten, although they also appear during the Ramesside era. High officials were most often rewarded for great service to the pharaoh with the "gold of honor," a special type of collar made up of gold disks strung on a cord, known as the *shebyu*. In depictions of this scene, the tomb owner generally appears before the pharaoh in one vignette, and then is shown again in a second, standing in front of an official who ties the *shebyu* collar around his neck. These ceremonies apparently took place in the treasury of the palace itself, and served both to reward the official and to redistribute royal wealth into the private sector. Afterwards, the tomb owner parades home, rejoicing in his newly elevated status; in at least one case, he is followed by men holding some sort of branch, thought by scholars to be a symbol of pleasure and praise.

For special service to the king an official might be awarded necklaces of gold in a public ceremony, and such an accolade would certainly be recorded in the recipient's tomb for perpetuity. Here, Paser, Governor and Vizier under Seti I and Ramesses II, is having the necklaces of gold beads – the "gold of honor" – tied around his neck (TT 106).

One example of such a reward scene appears in the tomb of Paser (TT 106). Another is found on the left focal wall in the transverse hall of Amenhotep-si-se's tomb chapel (TT 75); on the right wall is his biography, in which his appointment as Second Priest of Amun under Thutmose IV is recorded, along with scenes that illustrate this event. His installation apparently took place in the precinct of the Amun Temple at Karnak, shown by the unusual depiction of a pylon and a group of statues. Amenhotep-si-se, his head shaven in the traditional priestly style, holds a long staff. Facing him are women from his family, labeled as "singers of Amun"; his wife, Roy, holds a papyrus staff, symbol of the great goddess Hathor. Processions of men in the scene also carry papyrus stalks, or, in some cases, tall heads of lettuce, a plant associated with fertility and thus with the ithyphallic god Amun-Min because of its white sap, reminiscent of semen. Another interesting reward scene comes from TT 49, the tomb built for a Chief Scribe of Amun from the late 18th Dynasty, named Neferhotep, who is seen receiving the gold of honor from his king. A second scene depicts his wife, Merytre, being rewarded by the queen.

An important event in the life of any official was his promotion to high office, and some tombs include scenes directly related to the deceased's appointment and assumption of titles. Five viziers (e.g. Rekhmire, in TT 100) also include versions of a text describing their duties in their chapels. These are intriguing documents, which provide details both of decorum (for example, lower-ranking officials must stand rigid and speak in order of rank), of protocol (the Vizier must consult regularly with the Overseers of the Treasury, and report daily to the king; lower department heads could report wrongdoing, but only the Vizier could discipline other officials), and of philosophy (the Viziers are sternly admonished to be impartial in their judgments).

FESTIVAL SCENES

Religion permeated the lives of the Egyptians. The gods were responsible for bringing the universe into being, making sure that the daily cycle of the sun and the yearly cycle of the seasons continued as they should, that Egypt prospered and was protected from the chaotic foreign forces that surrounded it, and that humans were kept from danger in both their first and second lives. On the earthly plane, it was the king who was the principal intermediary between humans and the divine realm. The priests were his delegates, and ministered to the gods on his behalf.

Nubian delegates file in bearing tribute and make obeisance to pharaoh as part of a larger scene complex in the tomb of the Steward in the Southern City under Amenhotep III, Amenmesse (TT 89).

By the New Kingdom, and probably before, the blessed dead could also intercede with the gods on behalf of the living, and private piety, including ancestor cults and the worship of minor deities, was an essential part of the private religious landscape. Ancient sources, including a number of texts from the village of Deir el-Medina, inform us that Egyptians spent almost a sixth of their time, about 65 days a year, in such celebrations. Workers were given holidays, and the government administration provided extra rations. For the workmen of Deir el-Medina there were also some additional feasts, such as that of Amenhotep I, their "patron saint."

Communication with the gods and the blessed dead was easiest during feasts and festivals. For example, during certain celebrations, the statues of state gods left their temples to journey to other cult sites, hidden within their sacred traveling barks; during their journey, they could be petitioned by the populace. At festivals, music, dance, alcoholic beverages, and other intoxicating substances helped the participants reach the altered states of consciousness that would provide the illusion of communion between the human and divine realms.

A number of Theban tombs depict the celebration of important festivals, such as the New Year's and Montu festivals. Several tombs, mainly from the 18th Dynasty, contain scene complexes illustrating the Beautiful Feast of the Valley. This took place each year during the season of Shemu (harvest-time, from March to June), and was the period when the living could come closest to their beloved dead. A principal focus of this festival, during which the cult image of Amun was brought from its home at Karnak to the West Bank, was the worship of deceased and divinized kings, and of illustrious ancestors in general. Families would visit the necropolis and spend a day and night feasting and celebrating, hoping to

A group of elegant princesses (thought by some to be foreign) make offerings during the Sed Festival of Amenhotep III, a celebration of the rejuvenation of the king after 30 years of rule, from the tomb of Kheruef (TT 192) who was Steward of the Great Royal Wife, Tiye.

This productive orchard of a variety of fruit-bearing trees arranged around a pool forms the backdrop for two registers of men laden with offerings, in the tomb of Amenemhab (TT 85).

BELOW RIGHT
Under the watchful eye of an overseer with a whip, a group
of men carry and stack jars of wine inside a storehouse full
of local products, in an inner room of the chapel of the
tomb of Neferrenpet (TT 178), Scribe of the Treasury in
the Estate of Amun-Re.

communicate with their dead ancestors. Scenes illustrating this theme show the procession in which the bark of Amun and statues of the deceased kings were carried, as well as people visiting the tombs. Many banqueting scenes (see Chapter 6) are probably related to this festival as well.

In addition to the annual cycle of divine festivals, a king who reigned for 30 years or more could celebrate his Sed Festival, comprising a series of rituals designed to rejuvenate the monarch and ensure his fitness to continue on the throne. An unusual private representation of this festival, normally seen only in royal contexts, is found in the tomb of Kheruef (TT 192), Steward of the Great Royal Wife Tiye during the reign of Amenhotep III. Amenhotep III ruled for 38 years and observed three Sed Festivals, illustrations of two of which appear in the court of Kheruef's chapel. These are illuminating: in one, Amenhotep III and Tiye watch eight foreign princes offering gold and silver vessels, while female acrobats gyrate to the music of flute and voice, and other women clap to keep the rhythm. This is a wonderful scene, with the details of the dress and hairstyles of the women and the princes rendered in precise detail, and the surviving color hinting at the vibrancy of the original. In another, the king and queen enjoy watching a troupe of male dancers, who perform a stick-dance of a type still seen in Upper Egyptian villages today (see pp. 44–45). Key cult ceremonies are shown here, too, including the raising of the Djed pillar, symbol of the backbone of Osiris.

AGRICULTURE AND MANUFACTURE

Another important scene type depicts the tomb owner, seated or standing, overseeing the production and accounting of foodstuffs and manufactured items. In some cases, such scenes are part of a larger complex that includes an image of the king; in others the tomb owner appears to act independently, although always in actuality as a royal or divine delegate. On one level these scenes illustrate the duties of the tomb owner while alive, and generally relate to his titles; on another, they help to ensure the perpetual supply of goods for his cult (and in some cases for royal or divine cults as well). Larger complexes can include detailed depictions of various types of food production and processing, illustrations of the manufacture of different items, and the conveyance of the foods and goods to their destination.

Paintings devoted to agricultural activities and food production not only commemorated the duties for which an official would have been responsible during life, but also served to guarantee a supply of sustenance for the tomb owner in eternity. These scenes of harvesting, threshing, and winnowing are a detail from a much larger composition in the tomb of Menna (TT 69), more of which is shown on pp. 140–42.

The tomb of the vizier Rekhmire (TT 100) contains the most complete series of manufacturing scenes known. Images in the transverse hall show Rekhmire inspecting five registers of temple workshops and storerooms, including scenes of manufacture as well as baking, cooking, and possibly brewing beer. Most interesting here are royal statues in the form of the king in a variety of poses, along with sphinxes (see p. 151). A more extensive sequence spans eight registers on the left wall of the long passage leading to the cult niche.

SCENES OF FOOD PRODUCTION

The Nile Valley was a land of plenty, and food was generally abundant for the ancient Egyptians. Experts in the cultivation of grains (especially wheat and barley), legumes, fruits, and vegetables, they ate a variety of foodstuffs, with bread and beer as their staples. For meat, eggs, and milk, they domesticated a number of species of animals and birds, and supplemented their diet with fish, as well as wild animals and fowl. Vegetables and fruits in great variety were enjoyed by people of all ranks. The Egyptians seem to have eaten three meals a day, and the master of the house was responsible for making sure his family and servants were properly nourished.

Scenes of food production in the context of the tomb chapel served several purposes. First, they helped to guarantee that the deceased and his family would be well fed in the afterlife. They also related to the commemoration of the tomb owner's identity – scenes of agriculture, for example, are found most often in the tombs of royal or temple granary officials, who were responsible for the growing, harvesting, and accounting of grain; of high priests, who supervised all activities, including agriculture, for the holdings connected with their temples; or of viziers, who oversaw all activities connected with the royal estates. Depicting a successful agricultural cycle both honored the achievements of such bureaucrats on earth, and projected the image of a competent official into the eternal realm. All of these actions, carried out properly, also helped to sustain the Egyptian cosmos in its proper order, guaranteeing the regular annual cycle of the seasons and the daily cycle of the sun.

The Agricultural Cycle

The Theban tombs, like their predecessors from the earlier periods of Egyptian history, depict all the major phases of agriculture. Like many of the "earthly life" scene types, these are more common in the 18th Dynasty, and become rare in the Ramesside era. Farmers prepared the fields by breaking up the rich mud deposited by the yearly Nile flood using ox-drawn plows, with one man guiding the plow and a second leading the oxen. The next stage was to plant the seeds, which were carefully apportioned and accounted for by scribes. Using baskets to carry the seeds to the field, sowers threw handfuls into the furrows left behind by the plows. Goats or pigs were then driven into the fields to tread the seeds into the ground.

Harvesting was carried out by laborers who cut the ripe stalks of grain with sickles, then tied them into sheaves. The sheaves were carried to the threshing floor, where animal labor was again employed. After threshing came winnowing, when the heavier grains were separated from the chaff by tossing them in the air, a task for the most part done by women. Finally, the yield of the harvest was determined by measuring the heaps of processed grain and recording the amounts. The grain was stored in beehive-shaped granaries made of mud, with an opening in the top accessed by a ladder to load the grain and a door in the lower part to remove it.

Breadmaking

Following on from the sequence of the agricultural cycle is breadmaking, one of the earliest types of food production scene found in Egypt. The method followed throughout most of pharaonic history was as follows: first the grain was placed on a flat mortar of limestone and crushed with stone pestles. It was then reground with an ovoid or spherical pestle on a saddle quern, a flat rectangular stone that curved upward at the edges, resulting in a coarse flour generally containing a significant percentage of impurities such as sand and stone. This flour was collected in a small basin, then kneaded (either with the hands while kneeling on a low, flat surface, or in a vat using the feet) with water, yeast, and other ingredients such as spices, milk, butter, and eggs, and left to rise. The bread was then baked, either in a conical bread-mold or directly in a bread oven. A variety of breads of different shapes and consistency, as well as sweeter cakes and pastries, were enjoyed by the Egyptians. Actual New Kingdom examples of bread ovens have been found at Amarna and are also pictured in a side chamber in the tomb of Ramesses III. Conical in shape and about 1 meter high, they have a round hole at the top to release the smoke and a door at the bottom to tend the fire and turn the bread.

Brewing Beer

Beer was another nutritional staple of the Egyptian diet. It was traditionally made from wheat, which was soaked in water, dried, and then macerated until a bubbling mash resulted. This mash was put into a large vat together with yeast and crushed by treading. It was then left for a few days to ferment. Finally, it was sieved into a large container, and various flavors were added; at least 17 types of beer are known from texts. This beverage had a short shelf life and so was drunk, after being sieved again, soon after brewing.

Gardens and Orchards

The Egyptians were fond of a variety of vegetables, such as garlic, onions, cucumbers, leeks, and lettuce, and pulses, including chickpeas, lentils, and beans. These were planted in gardens, generally on private estates; fruit was grown in orchards.

PAGES 140–42
Menna, Scribe of the Fields of the Lord of the Two Lands in the 18th Dynasty, seated on a stool, watches as the various stages of the agricultural cycle are carried out, and the harvested grain is recorded and stored. The brightly colored scenes are full of lively details, such as two small girls tussling among the growing grain, and an official beating a wrongdoer in the upper register (TT 69).

PAGES 143–46
A troupe of male and female dancers whirl and make ritual gestures during the celebration of the Sed Festival of Amenhotep III, from the tomb of the Steward of Queen Tiye, Kheruef (TT 192). This finely carved relief is full of movement and rhythm.

Dates, sycomore figs, dom nuts, grapes (and raisins), and pomegranates were particular favorite fruits of the ancient Egyptians. One inscription informs us that there were over 100 kinds of sycomore trees.

Viniculture

Wine was a favorite beverage of the wealthy, and was particularly important for use in cult ceremonies. It is not surprising, therefore, that many of the Theban tombs include depictions of winemaking. The sequence began with gardeners collecting bunches of grapes from a thickly hung arbor. The grapes were carried in baskets to a treading floor lined with mortar and covered by a roof, similar to the presses used today in southern Europe, where they were pressed underfoot by workers who held on to ropes slung over the ceiling beams to keep their balance while they trampled the fruit. The juice flowed through pipes into a large basin, and the leftover skins and pips were put into canvas bags which were twisted to wring out the remaining juice. The must was then poured through cloth filters into vats where it was left to ferment, after which it was transferred into amphorae to mature. Spices or honey were added to some wines. At least six kinds of wine are known from ancient Egypt, including both red and white varieties. Then, as now, provenance and year were important, and were recorded carefully on the sealings of the jars in which the wine was stored, or on the jars themselves.

Animal Husbandry, Fishing, and Fowling

Cattle were the most essential domesticated animals in pharaonic Egypt, with cattle cults known as early as prehistoric times. The cow was a sacred animal, identified with Hathor, goddess of love and motherhood; the bull was a symbol of virility and power, and the king was associated with this animal throughout pharaonic history. Ownership of cattle was also an important measure of wealth, and royal cattle censuses were carried out from at least the Old Kingdom on.

Scenes showing the care of these creatures are found in a number of Theban tombs. In earlier Egyptian tombs, many aspects of cattle husbandry are depicted,

PAGES 147–49
Menkheperreseneb, the base of whose staff is just visible to the far left, observes the bustling activity in the manufacturing workshops that fall under his jurisdiction as High Priest of Amun (TT 86).

Men slaughter cattle and carry out various activities related to the production of wine (which was then stored in the rows of amphorae in the lower register), all under the watchful eye of Nebanum, who can be seen seated in the lower right of the image (TT 90).

from feeding, to herding, to milking; these are less common in the New Kingdom, but do continue to appear. Red meat was especially prized – roasted, grilled, baked, or cooked in stews. The foreleg was considered the choicest cut, and offered as a special part of the cult. Sheep and goats were also domesticated and consumed. Wild game birds, trapped or killed in desert hunts, were served as delicacies.

Several types of fowl, such as ducks and geese, were partially domesticated. These would be caught in clapnets, then kept and fattened before being killed and cooked, and could also be force-fed to produce an ancient Egyptian version of foie gras. Roasting and grilling were favorite methods of preparation for birds. Their eggs were also eaten in a variety of dishes. Fish were caught by teams of fishermen, who used large nets fitted with floats and sinkers or fished with rods and lines. The catch was filleted and often salted for longer-term storage, or grilled and eaten immediately.

Beekeeping

Honey is listed in Middle Kingdom cult menus (lists of food and other offerings that are found on false doors and tomb walls), but never appears on such lists in the New Kingdom. Wild honey was collected from the desert fringes from the Neolithic era on, and bees were kept at least as early as the Old Kingdom. However, we do see beekeeping represented in two Theban tombs (TT 93 and TT 100), and know that honey was used in religious rituals and for medicinal purposes. Bee hives were made from jars set sideways into a clay matrix. When it was time to collect the honey, the bees were smoked out with candles and the honeycombs collected. The honey was poured into special jars and the wax was collected separately.

SCENES OF MANUFACTURE

The ancient Egyptians were excellent craftsmen, able to work a variety of materials with great mastery. In New Kingdom Theban chapels, as in elite tombs of earlier periods, are scenes that depict a number of industrial activities, including the working of stone, wood, metal, and leather. We know from archaeological evidence that workshops were located close to one another in integrated complexes,

A group of royal statues in various poses, including sphinxes, occupies the middle register of this scene from the tomb of Vizier Rekhmire (TT 100). To the right are stores of goods from the royal workshops.

This image from a larger complex of manufacturing scenes in the inner room of the chapel of the 19th Dynasty tomb of Neferrenpet, Scribe of the Treasury in the Estate of Amun-Re, shows craftsmen occupied with a variety of tasks (TT 178). One man works on what appears to be a golden statue; others use bow-drills to perforate small beads. The level of detail in such scenes provides us with valuable information about the tools and techniques used by the ancient Egyptians in working a variety of materials.

and so in tomb scenes various types of materials are shown being worked side-by-side. Such scenes are also often found in concert with others depicting the collection, recording, and transport of the final products. Manufacture and food production might also be illustrated together, again reflecting the close connection between the two types of activities. The artists painted the processes of manufacture in such detail that we can learn a great deal about the materials and techniques used by the ancient Egyptians.

In addition to the factual details, the scenes are often full of life, with the workers laughing and joking among themselves. Accompanying texts sometimes specify that these activities are taking place in the royal or temple workshops, and that the objects being made in these scenes are specifically for the use of the king or god. The objects themselves can include royal statues or funerary shrines clearly destined for the king's burial. Such scenes, like so many others, served a dual purpose – they visibly commemorated the achievements and perpetuated the important activities supervised by the deceased during his career, and also guaranteed the eternal provisioning of the divine and royal cults, and so, by extension, the private mortuary cult.

Leatherworking

Leather was used for objects such as sandals and quivers. The material was first softened in large vats filled with some sort of oil (perhaps sesame) and in some cases tannin or alum, then stretched on the ground or on a wooden stand and beaten with stones, and the hair or fatty tissue scraped away. The leather was then dried, stretched, and placed on an inclined table to be cut out with a special knife.

Woodworking

Wood was a very versatile and invaluable material in ancient Egypt and was used to make many things, from tables and chairs for either daily life or funerary use (or both), to coffins and shrines. Egypt's woods are not good for carpentry, however, as they lack long stretches of trunk. For expensive items, coniferous woods, including cedar of Lebanon, and ebony, from which long planks could be cut, were imported from the northeast and the south respectively; other objects were patched together from smaller pieces of acacia or other native wood. New Kingdom carpenters used axes, with heads of bronze and hafts of wood, for chopping, and saws for cutting, attaching the wood to poles in the ground in order to keep their hands free for their work. Large knots and lumps were smoothed using adzes, again of bronze with

Metalworkers (above) and brick-makers (below) are among the detailed depictions of manufacture in the tomb of Rekhmire (TT 100). In the metalworking scenes, notice the foot-operated pot bellows and the craftsmen supporting a crucible. The brick-makers below fetch water from a pool in large pottery jars, tread the heaps of clay, and turn out bricks of uniform size by the use of a mold.

wooden shafts. To join large planks together, holes were bored and fitted with wooden dowels, or, less commonly, mortice-and-tenon joints were made. Wooden artifacts were often gessoed and then painted or gilded.

Goldsmithing and Metalworking

A number of tombs contain scenes showing the process of goldsmithing or the working of other metals. Again the paintings are so detailed that we can follow the individual stages of the manufacturing process. In the case of gold, the precious metal, in the shape of rings, is weighed carefully before being given to the artisan who will work it into its final form, all in the presence of a key official such as the vizier. In the next stage the gold was melted in crucibles over a fire, with workers sitting around it puffing into long pipes or using foot-operated bellows to fan the flames. Once the metal was molten, it was poured into molds and left to cool. The gold blocks were then given to smiths who hammered them into larger sheets using tools known from excavated examples to be of copper or limestone; their heads were covered with pieces of leather or cloth to prevent them from scratching the pliable metal.

Most gold was used for gilding or gold leaf, but solid gold objects were also made by casting in clay molds and by the lost-wax method. The pieces were then riveted or soldered together, and finally came the decoration with engraving or

Only the legs and the lower part of the bow belonging to a large figure of Ineni, Overseer of the Granary of Amun in the 18th Dynasty (TT 81), are visible in this desert hunt scene. His arrows have reached their targets, and his dog threatens a wounded hyena. Additional hunters can be seen in the register below.

chasing. A particularly interesting vignette in the tomb of Rekhmire (TT 100) shows the making of gold leaf to cover the wooden doors of the Temple of Amun at Karnak: after the metal was melted it was poured through a series of funnels into a mold, a method not known before the New Kingdom.

Textile Manufacture

One of the oldest industries in Egypt was the weaving of textiles. It was mainly Egyptian women who worked as weavers, although men did also perform this job. All cloth was made from plant fibers, primarily flax. The flax was prepared by first twisting it into balls; the fibers were then extracted by teasing them with combs, and these were soaked and wound onto spindles. In the New Kingdom, linen cloth was woven on simple vertical looms with square frames, working from the bottom up.

Weaving workshops were attached to the estates of the nobles, as well as to royal palaces and divine temples. The most extensive collection of clothing known from the New Kingdom comes, of course, from the tomb of Tutankhamun – his elaborately embroidered robes and simple but finely woven undergarments provide a sense of the expertise of the textile workers; the Asiatic influence seen in some garments also illustrates the cosmopolitan nature of Egypt during this era.

HUNTING IN THE DESERTS AND MARSHES

Key icons seen in many Theban tombs show the tomb owner hunting in the desert or fishing or fowling in the marshes. Such scenes date back to the Old Kingdom, and have long been recognized as apotropaic images that represent, on the most fundamental level, the eternal triumph of cosmic order over the forces of chaos, invoked here by the wild birds, fish, and animals of the marshes and deserts that lay at the margins of the Egyptian world. Nobles may also have participated in such hunts for sport, and certainly the images also relate in some way to the provisioning of the cult.

HUNTING IN THE DESERT

Depictions of desert hunts are known as far back as the Predynastic era, when they are found carved onto large slate cosmetic palettes. The animals targeted by the bows and arrows of the Egyptians included lions, wild cattle, ibex, gazelles, and hyenas. Hunting dogs often assisted their masters. It was the king himself who was first – and most often – shown leading the desert hunt, and many scenes and inscriptions emphasize the importance of this activity in the royal realm. From the Old Kingdom on, members of the high elite are also seen engaging in hunting. Although such scenes were in part symbolic, to ward off chaos, in reality desert hunts would also have served to provide food for the table. Hunting would also have been good training for battle, proof of the monarch's (or official's) might, as well as being simple sport.

Thutmose III was an especially avid hunter; his son, Amenhotep II, was extremely proud of his athletic prowess. It is perhaps a reflection of this love of hunting that the majority of desert hunt scenes at Thebes date to the reigns of these

two kings. Amenhotep III was also fond of the chase, and commemorated some of his greatest hunts on scarabs, such as the killing of 96 out of 170 wild cattle (after they had been corralled into a walled enclosure with a ditch) and the fact that he slew 102 lions during the first 10 years of his reign. Tutankhamun recorded his success in hunting a troop of young ostriches on a golden fan found in his tomb.

Nobles were equally fond of desert hunts. In the tomb of the Royal Scribe Userhat (TT 56), we see the tomb owner in his horse-drawn chariot, drawing his bow as he speeds across the desert landscape. Desert animals such as gazelles and rabbits fall under the rain of arrows he unleashes, while a small fox tangles himself in a desert plant as he tries to escape. The artist has been very successful in rendering movement and detail, and in conveying the natural landscape. Perhaps such a hunt took place in reality, but in the context of the tomb, this icon serves mainly to keep the chaotic world represented by these animals and their desert world at bay, and to promise eternal youth and strength to Userhat.

FISHING AND FOWLING IN THE MARSHES

Like the desert hunt, scenes of the tomb owner fishing with a harpoon and fowling with a throwstick are popular from the Old Kingdom on, and again symbolize the triumph of order over chaos, while simultaneously depicting a sport and providing food for the cult table. Such scenes are also full of erotic imagery, and thus help to guarantee the perpetual rebirth of the deceased.

Fishing and fowling icons are often seen in the form of symmetrically placed, large-scale mirror images of the tomb owner standing in a papyrus skiff, usually accompanied by members of his family, particularly his wife and daughters. Both fishing and fowling took place in the marshes, which were located in the Delta and along the fringes of the cultivation, where the water from the receding Nile flood would collect each year. In the fishing scenes, the deceased uses a harpoon to spear large fish, generally tilapia (perch) or Lates, and lift them from the canal or river, which the artist shows streaming around them to form a sort of "mountain" of water. The target of the hunt can also be a hippopotamus (most often attested from the reign of Thutmose III), totem animal of the god Seth and embodiment of chaos. When hunting birds, the tomb owner generally wielded a throwstick, sometimes in the shape of a snake, in one hand, while holding decoy birds in his other.

Some of the most famous New Kingdom examples of fishing and fowling icons are found in the tomb of Menna (TT 69); these are substantially intact apart from the faces of the tomb owner, which have been removed, most likely by later iconoclasts. The two images have been integrated into a single scene, placed on the right-hand wall of the long passage. In both images, Menna wears a transparent short-sleeved tunic over a kilt, with a floral collar around his neck. In the fowling scene he holds a throwstick with one hand and a group of decoy birds in the other; in the fishing image he leans forward to spear two large fish that emerge from the canal in a hill of water.

The two scenes are united by this water, and by the clump of papyrus teeming with birds and butterflies above it. The artist has added a touch of whimsy in the form of a cat that flushes the birds out of their nests, and an ichneumon that climbs up a papyrus stalk. The canal below Menna's papyrus skiffs is populated with fish and birds of various kinds, water plants, and a crocodile, which lurks beneath the prows, all painted in beautiful detail. Menna is accompanied by two men, perhaps one or more of his sons, his wife, and several additional women, dressed in their best finery and carrying marsh plants and birds, all erotically charged symbols.

PAGES 157–58
The army commander Amenemhab faces an enormous hyena in a scene of hunting in the desert above a doorway in his tomb (TT 85). Such scenes were both representations of a favorite sport of the Egyptians – one that would have displayed courage and military prowess – and also had symbolic connotations of the triumph of order over the forces of chaos.

PAGES 159–62
The Royal Scribe and Child of the Nursery, Userhat, wields his bow and drives his chariot into a melee of fleeing and wounded desert animals, including rabbits and a herd of gazelles (TT 56).

Menna appears twice in this scene of fishing and fowling in the marshes in his tomb (TT 69), accompanied and assisted by members of his family. Dressed in a white gauzy robe and broad collar, he stands on a papyrus skiff and brings down waterfowl with a snake-shaped throwstick (left) and catches fish with a spear (right). The different types of fish and waterfowl are rendered in precise detail.

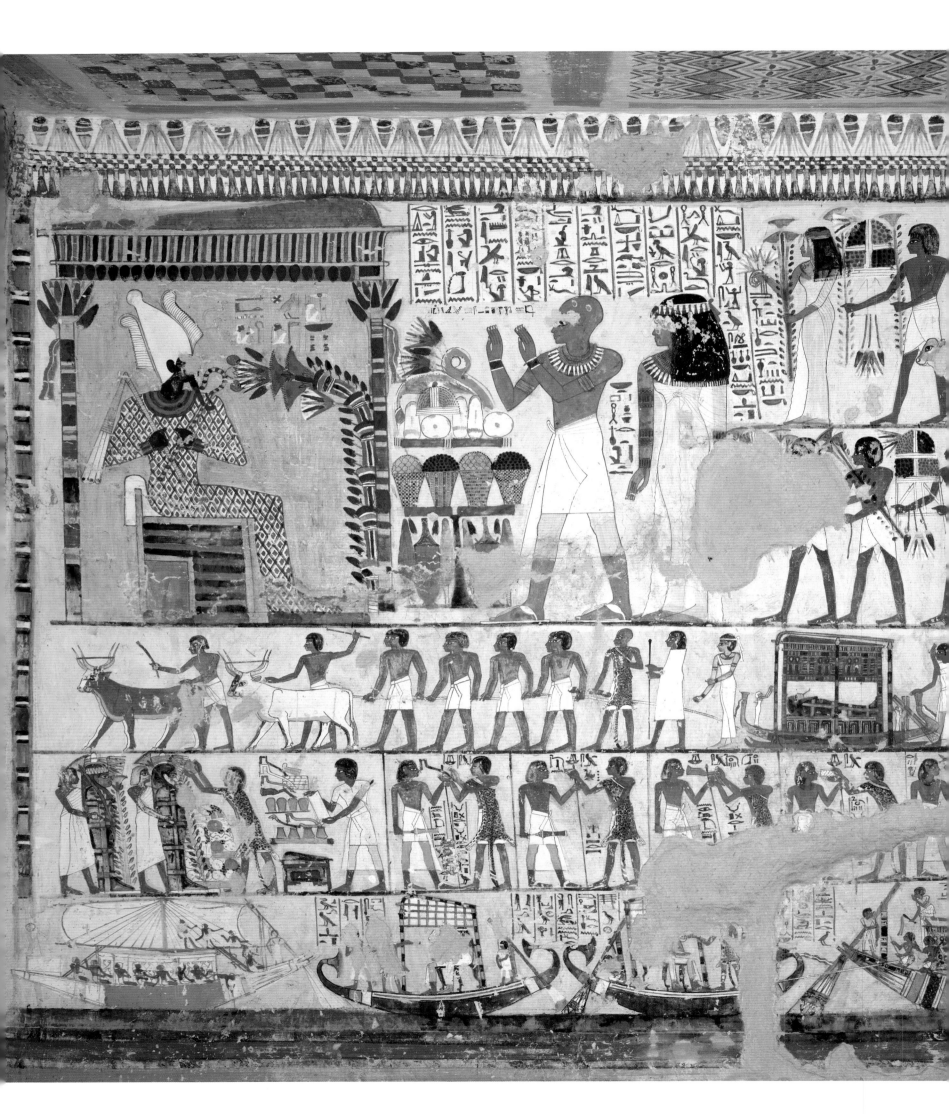

The north wall of the mid-18th Dynasty tomb of Pairy
(TT 139), a priest during the reign of Amenhotep III, is
decorated with a full complex of scenes related to life after
death. In the bottom register is the pilgrimage to Abydos.
Above this, the Opening of the Mouth ritual is carried out
on a number of statues of the tomb owner; the funeral
procession itself is shown in the next register. The top of the
wall shows the arrival of Pairy and his wife Henutnefert,
accompanied by offering bearers, into the realm of Osiris.

CHAPTER FIVE

FROM DEATH TO ETERNAL LIFE

An essential category of scenes found in the Theban tombs relates to the
preparations for, and celebration of, the funeral itself. The process of burial began
with the mummification of the body and a pilgrimage (either real or symbolic) to
the sacred site of Abydos, followed by the funeral procession and the rites at
the tomb itself, including the cult meal. After the funeral, the deceased, now
transformed into a blessed spirit (an *akh*) could meet and worship the gods.
Complementing these scenes, and becoming more common in later tombs until
they overtake representations of earthly life, are images related to a corpus of texts
known as the Netherworld Books. These helped to guide the deceased during
his perilous journey from death to resurrection, and illuminate the ideal eternal
life. Together, these scenes and texts allow us to explore Egyptian concepts of death
and resurrection.

THE JOURNEY FROM DEATH TO RESURRECTION

Many New Kingdom Theban tombs preserve representations of the ceremonies
and rituals connected with all stages of the funeral, often grouped together,
although in reality they did not occur at the same time. In the earlier 18th Dynasty,
these appear most often in the chapels, generally in the long hall leading to the cult
niche where they could be seen by visitors to the tomb; from the reign of Amenhotep III on, they can also spill over into the transverse hall. In the 19th and 20th
Dynasties, they become even more common, and are also found in the burial
chamber (especially at Deir el-Medina). The details vary a great deal from one
tomb to another, as does the choice of which scenes to include and the order in
which they are arranged, but the basic elements can be reconstructed from the
most complete examples.

Representations of the funeral from the early part of the 18th Dynasty follow
the patterns set out in previous periods, and may even include images of rituals that
were no longer carried out. After the reign of Thutmose IV, some of the older rites
were omitted, and the funeral was shown in a single sequence. During the Ramesside period, representations of this event became even more simplified, with only
the essential vignettes depicted. The most complete representation of the funeral
from the New Kingdom is found in the long hall of TT 100, the tomb of the vizier
Rekhmire (see pp. 19–21).

MUMMIFICATION

Immediately after death, the first stage in a successful transition to the afterlife
was the proper preparation of the body, a procedure carried out by professional
embalmers. The journey of the body to the location where the mummification
rituals were performed is seen in earlier tombs, but in New Kingdom scenes, it is

only the final stages of the process that are shown. These images are generally found in burial chambers, and can appear in a number of variations.

Most commonly, a priest wearing a jackal mask that identifies him with the god of mummification, Anubis, leans over the body of the deceased, which has been laid on a funeral couch with the legs and sometimes the head and tail of a lion. Known from the earliest periods of Egyptian history, such embalming beds protected the deceased by associating him or her with the strength of the lion. This animal was also linked with the eastern and western horizons, and thus to the daily cycle of the sun that was in turn the guarantor of resurrection. Often, the couch is flanked by Isis (at the foot of the couch) and Nephthys (at the head), sometimes in human form and sometimes in the guise of birds of prey called kites. The presence of these two goddesses identifies the deceased with their brother (and Isis's husband) Osiris, whose body they reassembled and revivified after his murder and dismemberment by Seth (see p. 67). In some instances, the Anubis-priest simply bends over the mummy, presumably chanting prayers. In others, he performs the Opening of the Mouth ceremony (see below), by which the mummy was rendered capable of functioning in the next world. Texts inscribed around these scenes are often spells spoken by the embalmer, who promises protection for the body of the deceased.

PILGRIMAGES

Included with depictions of the funeral are often scenes that show the deceased, in some cases with his wife or mother, making a pilgrimage to a sacred cult site, generally one that was associated with Osiris. When Osiris was killed and dismembered by his brother Seth, his body parts were scattered over all of Egypt. Each place where a part was recovered by Isis and Nephthys became sacred to the god.

PAGES 169–70
This detail from the funeral procession in TT 54, which was originally built and decorated for a Sculptor of Amun named Huy and later usurped by a Purification Priest, Kenro, includes the coffin, invisible within a shrine (above), and the canopic chest, protected by a priest wearing the jackal mask of Anubis (below). In the lower register is also a group of mourning women.

A priest wearing an Anubis-mask performs the Opening of the Mouth ritual on the mummy of Nakhtamun (TT 335), who lies on a bed with feet in the shape of lion's paws. The goddesses Nephthys and Isis pour libations at his head and feet to purify him. Below the couch are vessels containing unguents, a mirror, a shabti box, and a chest on a sledge containing his embalmed viscera.

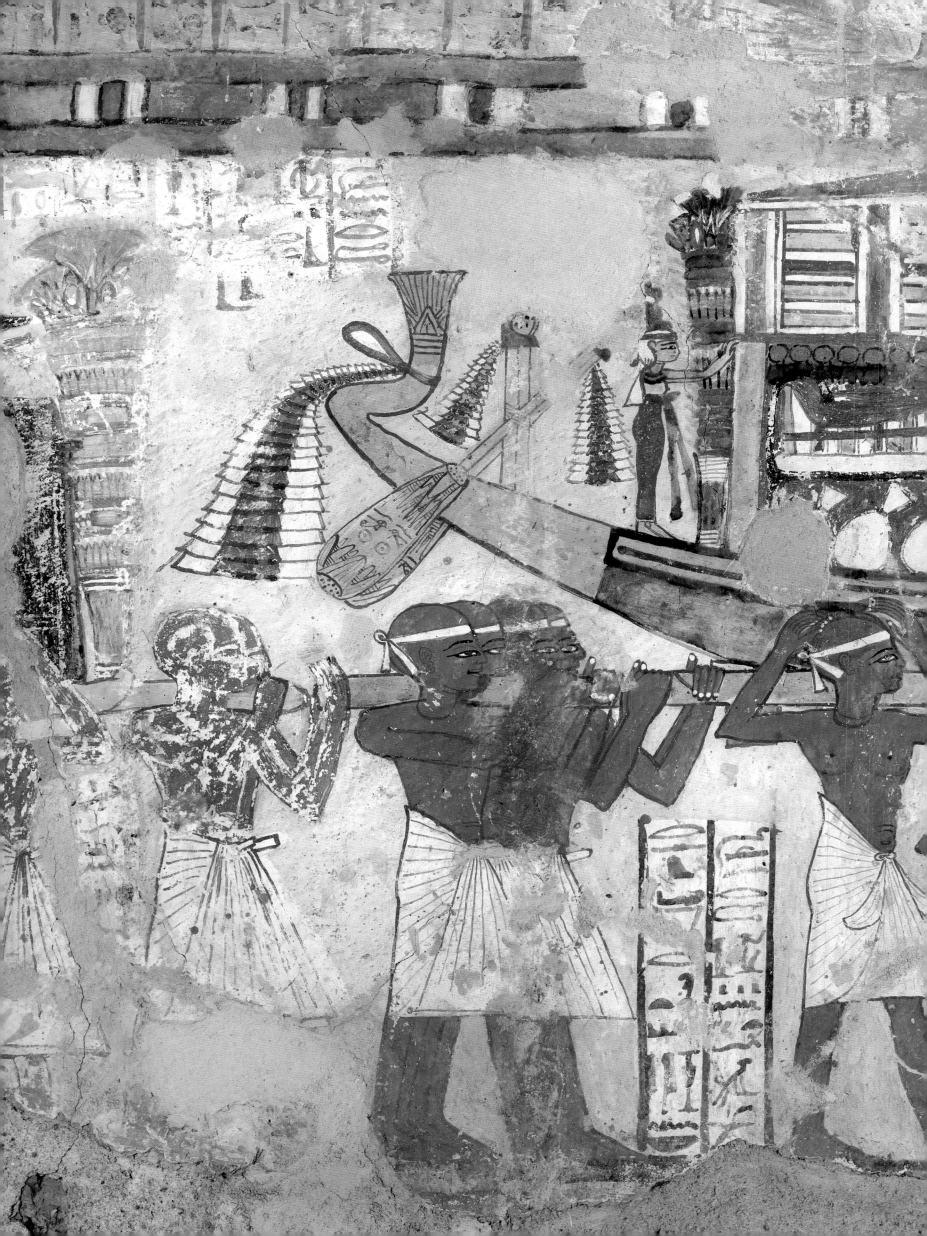

A journey by boat is often depicted in Theban tombs. It might represent either the pilgrimage to the sacred site of Abydos, principal cult place of Osiris, or the transport of the mummy across the Nile from the East Bank to the necropolis. In this example from the tomb of Rekhmire (TT 100) the upper ship is being rowed by a crew of oarsmen.

PAGES 171–72
The coffined mummy of Nakhtamun, Chief of the Altar in the Ramesseum under Ramesses II, set within a shrine and placed on a sacred bark, is carried on the shoulders of eight men. Nakhtamun's son acts as the chief cult celebrant: wearing the leopard-skin robe of a priest, he offers incense to his deceased father (TT 341).

Many of these sites became known as *Per-usir*, or House of Osiris, which was transformed into Busiris in Greek and then Abusir in Arabic.

The most common pilgrimage site was Abydos, Osiris's principal cult place. It was at Abydos that, according to Egyptian mythology, Isis and Nephthys found their brother's head. All Egyptians wished to travel to the sacred site, either at some point during their lives or after death, to be eternally reborn with the god. Ideally, this visit to Abydos would coincide with the god's annual festival, which took place over a period of 14 days in the first month of the flood. During this feast, the death and resurrection of Osiris were ritually re-enacted, with mystery plays and processions down the Great Wadi that led from the floodplain to the cemetery where the first kings of Egypt (*c.* 3000 BC) had been buried. During the Middle Kingdom, a millennium later, one of these early royal tombs had been identified as the grave of Osiris, and became a focus of the ceremonies.

The easiest way to travel from one part of Egypt to another was by boat along the country's main thoroughfare, the Nile. Pilgrimage scenes in the Theban tombs therefore show the deceased being transported by boat, in the form of a mummy or statue, to the cult site, then returning as a resurrected spirit. The boat in which the deceased travels takes the shape of a papyrus skiff (which also has overtones of the marshy landscape of creation), towed by a second boat. On the journey north – or downstream – from Thebes, the lead boat is rowed by a crew of oarsmen; on the way back south, the sails are raised to catch the prevailing winds.

It is believed by most scholars that, at least by the New Kingdom, it was not necessary for the body or statue of the deceased physically to travel to the cult site

and back. Instead, the pilgrimage could be re-enacted ritually as part of the funeral rites, with the mummy carried to areas within the necropolis that were identified with Abydos or other cult sites.

FUNERAL PROCESSION

On the day of the funeral, the mummy would be taken from the embalmers and borne to the tomb, as the focal point of a procession. It could be transported simply within its inner coffin, or it might be nested inside a full set of coffins and shrines. Generally supported on a base in the form of a boat, the entire assemblage was placed on a sledge. Figures of one or two women (representing Isis and Nephthys) are often shown flanking the coffins within the shrine. It is probable that part of the embalming process was performed on the East Bank, so the procession might include placing the mummy on a boat and ferrying it across the Nile to the necropolis. The symbolism of this trip across the Nile can also be conflated with the pilgrimage scenes. For the procession to the river, and from the river to the tomb,

Tiny figures of Isis and Nephthys protect the mummy of the Steward in the Estates of Horemheb and Amun, Roy, who is nested inside his coffin and shrine, the whole assemblage resting on a base in the shape of a boat. The chief priest offers incense and makes a libation, while Roy's wife, Nebettawy, leads the mourners in her husband's funeral procession (TT 255).

the sledge was either dragged by oxen or carried by male friends and relatives of the deceased (the precursors of our pall bearers). In some cases, it could be placed on a wheeled cart.

A second sledge, carrying a strange object known as the *tekenu,* is frequently depicted in these scenes. Often represented as a bundle wrapped in an animal skin, but sometimes with a human head poking out of the top, and in at least one instance in the form of a man lying in the fetal position, the meaning of this mysterious item is a matter of scholarly debate. Some believe that the bundle contained material left over from the mummification process that would have been gathered together and saved for ritual burial, as anything that could contain fragments of the individual was considered sacred. Others think the placenta was saved from birth and included in the burial, or that this object is a reference to some sort of ancient human sacrifice, only practiced in the very earliest periods of Egypt's history.

Another essential item of funerary equipment was the canopic chest, which held the jars that contained the embalmed viscera removed from the body during

This wonderful detail from the funeral procession of Ramose
(TT 55) depicts a crowd of mourning women, with tears
running down their faces, many of whom cup their hands
to ululate in an expression of grief (for a view of more of
the procession, see pp. 16–18).

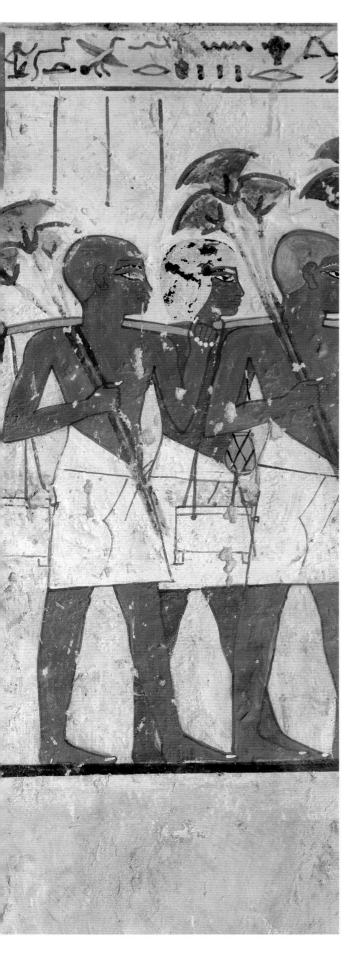

ABOVE RIGHT
In the tomb of Userhat (TT 51), a High Priest, mourning women kneel and throw dust over their heads while the chief cult celebrant, wearing a leopard-skin robe, offers incense to the deceased. A second figure directly behind him pours a libation.

mummification. This chest was also often placed on a sledge and pulled along as part of the funeral procession. Additional offering bearers would carry boxes and chests containing the various objects, offerings, and items of furniture that would be placed in the tomb.

A number of tombs depict groups of primarily female mourners raising their arms in gestures of grief. According to Herodotus, the female relatives of the deceased would smear their heads and faces with dust and beat their exposed breasts. The leader of this group is generally the tomb owner's wife, identified with the goddess Isis. Sometimes she is accompanied by a second principal mourner, representing Nephthys. In some cases they follow a priest dressed in a short enveloping cloak that reaches to the knee, similar to a garment worn by the king during his Festival of Rejuvenation, the Sed. Most processions include the *sem* priest, shown with a shaved head and wearing a leopard skin. Associated with Horus, the eldest son and heir of Osiris, it was the *sem* priest who would preside over the ceremonies at the tomb. A lector priest, responsible for reading out the cult ritual, may also be depicted; he can be recognized by his kilt and sash, and by the scroll he carries.

Seen in a number of tombs are dancers known as the *Muu*. These ritual performers are easily recognized by their distinctive tall headdresses, evidently made from papyrus plants. They are thought to have participated in the funeral at several specific points, joining the procession as it reached the edge of the necropolis and emerging from the "Hall of the Muu" to greet the mummy within its

coffins. A recent theory suggests that these male dancers represented divine gatekeepers and ferrymen, who welcomed the deceased to the cemetery on behalf of the Goddess of the West and guided the mummy to the tomb. They were also part of a group of mythical beings known as the Followers of Re, who traveled with the sun god on his journey through the Netherworld.

RITES AT THE TOMB

The goal of the procession was the tomb itself, represented in the decoration as a small building with a door. This might be topped with a pyramid, especially after the reign of Amenhotep III, and can also be shown as built into the side of a mountain, as the tombs were in reality. A number of important rituals were carried out upon the arrival of the mummy at the tomb. Known as the *sakhu* rites, these were designed to assist with the transformation of the deceased into an *akh*, a blessed spirit (see p. 66).

The mummy was set upright on a mound or patch of sand, perhaps representing the primeval hill of creation. An unguent cone was frequently placed on the mummy's head. The female mourners would come near, and the deceased's wife, as Isis, would kneel at the mummy's feet and throw dust on her head. Often the depiction of grief is touchingly detailed and evocative, with tears springing from the women's eyes.

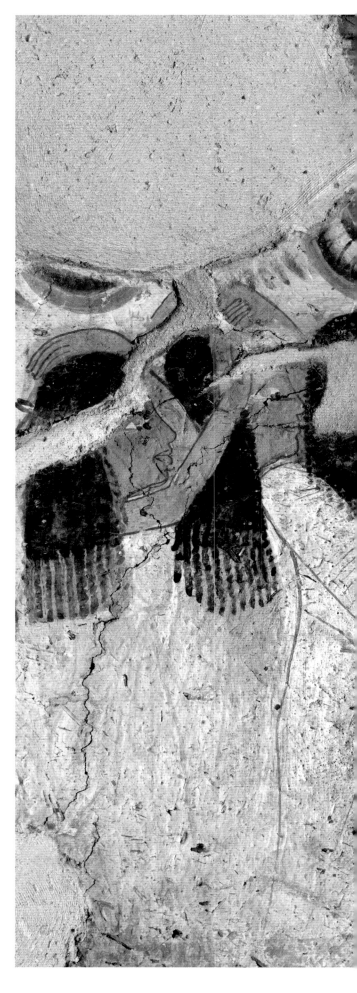

ABOVE LEFT
Wearing the jackal mask of Anubis, a priest supports the mummy of Roy (TT 255) while the Opening of the Mouth ceremony is carried out to restore the deceased's faculties.

A priest recites the proper prayers while another offers incense and libations to two mummies in this scene from the tomb of Userhat (TT 51).

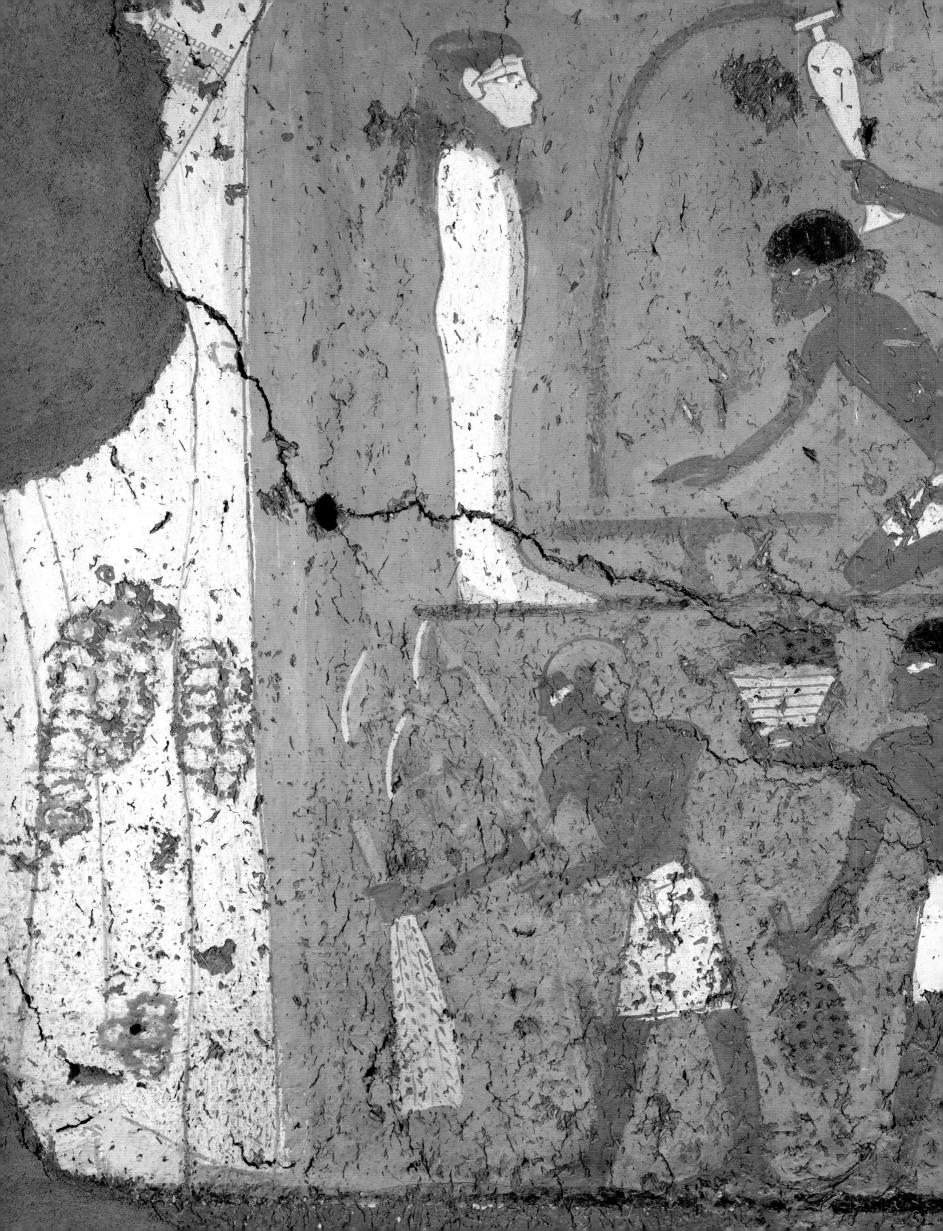

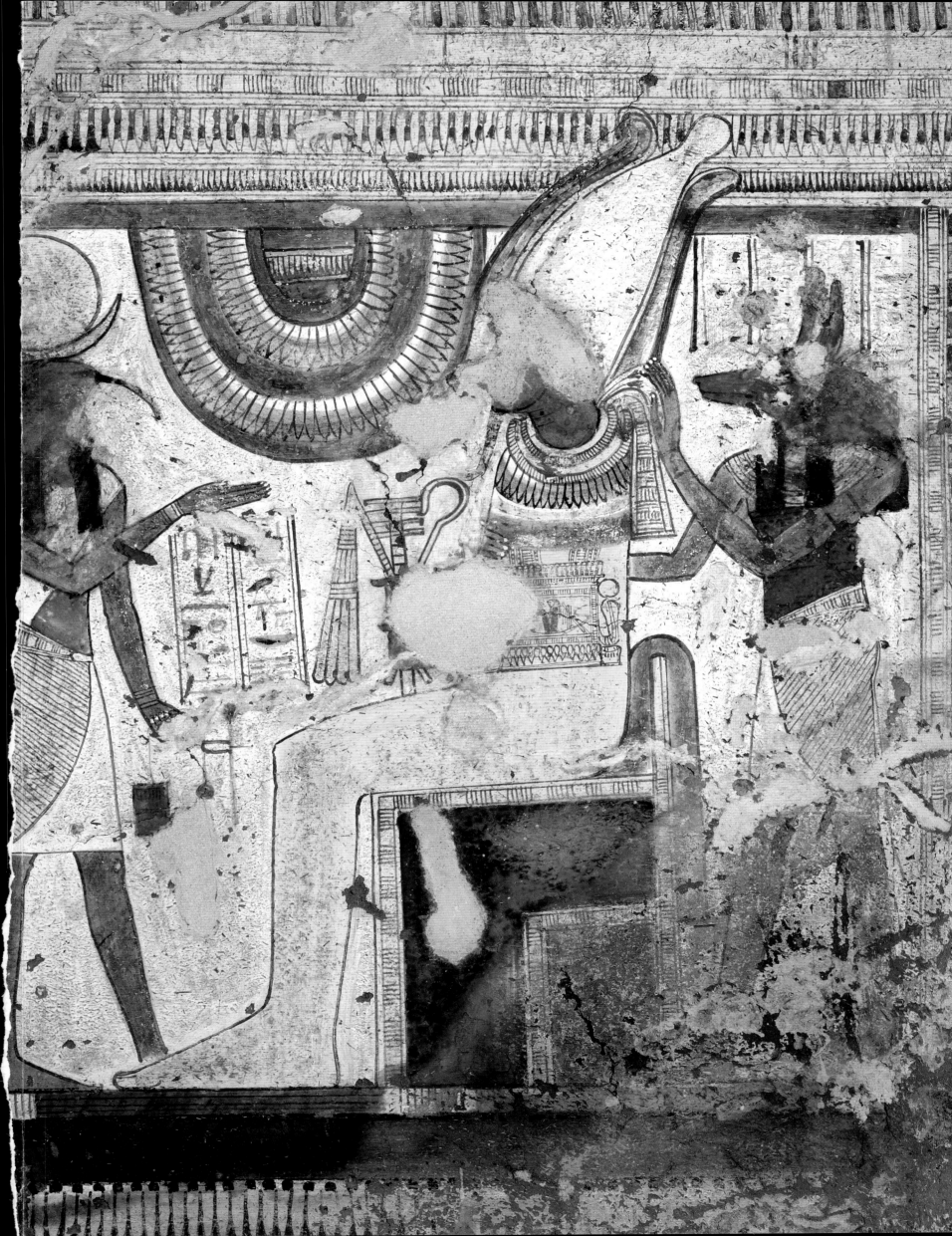

Khonsu, the son of the royal artisan Sennedjem, performs the Opening of the Mouth ceremony on his father's mummy (TT 1). Touching the mummy's lips with an adze and other tools allowed it to eat, drink, and speak once more and ideally it was the eldest son of the deceased who would carry out this important ritual.

The Opening of the Mouth

The principal ceremony depicted in front of the tomb was the Opening of the Mouth, by which the mummy's necessary faculties (sight, hearing, smell, and taste) were magically restored in order for the deceased to be able to benefit from the offering cult. Based on a ritual designed to animate statues so that they could function as receptacles for the *ka*, this became the fundamental ceremony in which effigies of any sort, including the mummy, were prepared to receive the cult, and was thus an essential part of the funeral. When performed on the mummy, it is thought that this also signaled the moment at which various incorporeal aspects of the person could rejoin the body.

The Opening of the Mouth was an elaborate ceremony. The words recited during this ritual are recorded first in the Pyramid Texts (see below); by the New Kingdom, these had been expanded and broken down into 75 vignettes. Most often shown officiating at this event in the Theban tombs was the *sem* priest (ideally the eldest son of the deceased), who performed a number of rites. The key rite was the touching of the mummy's lips with a model adze and other ritual tools, so that, as a repository for the deceased's *ka*, it could eat, drink, and speak. One Egyptologist has suggested that this part of the ritual was connected with the clearing of the baby's mouth at birth. A priest wearing the mask of Anubis might also be shown assisting with this rite, or performing it on the mummy as it lay on an embalming couch (see pp. 25 and 168). The adze was also used to touch the eyes, ears, and nostrils, to restore all the senses, all accompanied by the chanting of the appropriate spells.

Other rites

Another important rite celebrated at the funeral was the sacrifice of a bull and the offering of the choicest cuts of meat to the deceased. Libations were also poured over the mummy to purify it; it was offered incense to bring it closer to the divine realm; and it was anointed with perfumed oils and unguents. Additional food and drink were presented, and the *hetep di nesu* offering prayer recited. (See Chapter 6 for more detail on cult rituals and offering meals.)

BURIAL

After the proper rites had been performed, the mummy, with all its equipment, was lowered down the shaft to the burial chamber and carefully placed in what was intended to be its resting place for all eternity. The body was laid inside its nest of coffins and enclosed in a series of shrines; the canopic chest and other burial

PAGES 180–82
In this complex of scenes from the tomb of Djehutynefer, Royal Scribe and Overseer of the Treasury under Amenhotep II (TT 80), libations are poured, cattle slaughtered, and offerings made to the mummy.

PAGES 183–84
The ruler of the Netherworld, Osiris, sits enthroned in a kiosk attended by Anubis, god of embalming, who stands behind him, and Thoth, god of wisdom and writing, who stands before him, in a scene from the 19th Dynasty tomb of the High Priest Userhat (TT 51). On the left are registers showing groups of various gods within shrines.

Roy and his wife, Nebettawy, raise their hands in adoration of a god. Nebettawy, who was a Chantress of Amun, carries a sistrum (ritual rattle), a sacred *menat* necklace, and a papyrus plant, all of which were used in religious ceremonies (TT 255).

equipment, including furniture and food offerings, were placed nearby. Additional rituals would have been performed, and then the chamber would have been sealed, ideally to be opened only if another body was added later. The final rites would have been carried out inside the upper chapel, and the mourners would have enjoyed a banquet at which they could magically commune with the transformed spirit of the newly resurrected deceased. The burial itself is not represented as part of the repertoire of scenes.

THE TOMB OWNER AND THE GODS

After the Opening of the Mouth ceremony, the deceased was able to function in the next world and could begin the journey to eternal life. Many funeral sequences (as well as other scenes) include a meeting of the tomb owner, often accompanied by his wife or mother, with Osiris or Anubis, with the Mistress of the Sycomore or with the Goddess of the West. In later tombs, additional gods and goddesses such as Re-Horakhty, Ma'at, and Ptah, might also be represented.

OSIRIS

The meeting of the deceased with Osiris is often seen in association with the funeral, but can also occur in other contexts. It could only take place after the funeral ceremonies, however, as it was necessary for the deceased to have begun the transition to the state of blessedness. In these scenes, Osiris sits on a throne or stands, wearing his typical uniform of mummy bandages and tall white crown flanked by the ostrich plumes of *ma'at*. Often he is shown within a shrine, similar to the kiosk in which the king sits in the earthly life scenes. The tomb owner stands before Osiris, frequently with his arms raised in a gesture of worship, or performing cult rituals.

Kenro, a priest, presents a burnt offering in a brazier to the goddess Hathor in the form of a sacred cow, as she emerges from the Theban mountains (TT 54); a table of offerings stands between them.

GODDESS OF THE WEST

In many tombs, the deceased is welcomed after the funeral by the Goddess of the West. Often identified with Hathor, she is represented in earlier tombs as a woman wearing a tight-fitting, archaic dress, with the hieroglyph for her name – a standard topped by the word for "west," *imentet,* and a Horus falcon – on her head. In later tombs she is seen in the form of a cow (associated with Hathor) or a cobra, emerging from the rocky landscape of the Theban massif. The deceased stands before her, making offerings of food, drink, or incense, in order to pacify her and ensure that she will offer her protection in the afterlife.

OPPOSITE
In this famous scene from the tomb of Sennedjem (TT 1) the tomb owner and his wife, having emerged from the tomb, kneel and raise their arms in supplication to the goddess who takes the form of a tree, with her legs and feet as the trunk and roots and branches emerging from her body. In response to Sennedjem and Iynefer, the tree goddess holds a mat on which loaves of bread, drink, and vegetables have been placed.

RIGHT
Ameneminet, a priest during the Ramesside period, rasies his hands in a gesture of worship before Osiris, ruler of the Netherworld, on the left, and Ma'at, the embodiment of truth and justice, on the right (TT 277).

PAGES 191–94
Nakhtamun, a royal artisan and priest of the local cult of Amenhotep I, is shown on one wall of his burial chamber, with various different gods: (from left to right) Nakhtamun, in the leopard skin of a priest, pouring libations to Osiris; the divinized Amenhotep I with the goddesses Buto and Neith; the composite goddesses of childbirth, Tawaret (as Tahenutsekhen) and Anuket; and Nakhtamun and his wife paying homage to Re-Horakhty (TT 335).

PAGES 195–97
In this scene from the tomb of the royal artisan Irunefer (TT 290), the tomb owner's parents, their age indicated by their white hair, pay homage to Ptah, the patron deity of craftsmen. Irunefer himself kneels and offers a figure of the goddess Ma'at.

MISTRESS OF THE SYCOMORE

Common in Ramesside tombs are images that show the deceased worshipping the Great Goddess (identified with different deities, including Hathor and Nut) in her various guises. From at least the Old Kingdom, an important aspect of the Great Goddess was the Mistress of the Sycomore. A number of tombs, especially at Deir el-Medina, show the tomb owner and his wife emerging from the tomb to make supplication to the tree goddess, who offers them food and drink, helping to ensure their sustenance in the world beyond the earth.

OTHER GODS

A number of other gods are found represented in the New Kingdom tombs of Thebes. For example, several tombs include images of the tomb owner worshipping the falcon-headed Re-Horakhty, an incarnation of the sun god as a syncretization of Re and Horus. The patron god of artisans and tutelary deity of Memphis, Ptah, represented as a man wrapped in mummy bandages and wearing a tight-fitting skull cap, is found in several tombs at Deir el-Medina. Also popular was the Memphite

In the underground chamber of Senenmut (TT 353), Chief Steward during the reign of Hatshepsut, the walls are covered with beautifully carved texts from the *Book of the Dead*. Visible in the center of the wall is a false door, which would have formed the focus of the cult. (For another view of the chamber, see pp. 77–78; and for the astronomical ceiling, see pp. 111–13.)

Roy, Steward in the Estates of Amun and Horemheb, is led by the falcon-headed god Horus into the presence of Osiris (not shown here) in the Hall of Judgment (TT 255).

funerary god Sokar, who could also be represented as the composite deities Ptah-Sokar or Ptah-Sokar-Osiris. The goddess who embodied the proper order of the Egyptian cosmos, Ma'at, was another occasional choice, as were the members of the Theban triad: Amun-Re, his consort Mut, and their son Khonsu.

NETHERWORLD BOOKS

Appearing in some earlier New Kingdom tombs, and gaining in importance over time, are scenes derived from a corpus of illustrated texts known collectively to Egyptologists as the Netherworld Books. These developed over time from verses first seen in the Old Kingdom in the form of Pyramid Texts, collections of hieroglyphic spells that were inscribed on the walls of royal burial suites. These Pyramid Texts were designed to ensure the successful journey of the deceased king, and later also his queens, to the afterlife, as well as to guarantee their sustenance there. Included in the spells are incantations to protect the deceased from dangerous magical creatures; recitations of the offering and "resurrection" rituals related to the funeral (spoken by Horus for the king as an incarnation of his father Osiris); and other spells covering a variety of other aspects. All the different afterlife traditions are mentioned: the king's journey to join the stars; his identification with Osiris; and his relationship to the sun god.

In the late Old Kingdom and Middle Kingdom a new corpus of spells is found, mainly painted on the coffins of the elite. Known as the Coffin Texts, these were based on the Pyramid Texts, and contain many of the same spells, but expand on the journey of the *ba* through the heavens and Netherworld. New spells seen here belong to the category of guides to the Netherworld. Accompanied by maps of this mythical landscape, these spells helped the deceased journey safely to the afterlife.

A number of new texts related to life after death are attested from the New Kingdom. For the elite, the earliest and most common of these is the *Book of Coming forth by Day*, or the *Book of the Dead*, which contains spells from both the

This vignette from the tomb of Nebamun and Ipuky (TT 181) shows the great god Osiris, his hands protruding from his mummy wrappings to grasp the crook and flail. Seated behind him are the Four Sons of Horus. These were canopic deities who protected the embalmed viscera of the deceased: human-headed Imsety; baboon-headed Hapy; falcon-headed Qebehsenuef; and the jackal-headed Duamutef (of whom only the legs and a fragment of the head are visible).

Pyramid and Coffin Texts, as well as new incantations. The Middle Kingdom Netherworld guides develop into the *Books of the Underworld* (primarily the *Book of the Amduat;* the *Book of Gates;* and the *Book of Caverns*), seen first in royal tombs of the 18th and 19th Dynasties. There are also several later additions to this tradition.

THE BOOK OF THE DEAD (THE BOOK OF COMING FORTH BY DAY)

Called by the ancient Egyptians the *Peret em Heru,* or *Coming Forth by Day,* and known colloquially as the *Book of the Dead,* this extensive collection of spells (around 200) is most commonly preserved in the form of papyrus scrolls found in private tombs. The text is inscribed in vertical columns and interspersed with carefully painted illustrations. The heading of each spell, the rubric, is usually written in red ink. Spells from this corpus can also be found on coffins, mummy shrouds, mummy bandages, selected funerary objects, and on the walls of tombs. Illustrations and texts from some of these spells (or chapters, as they are also called) appear in tomb decoration of the 18th Dynasty; in the Ramesside period they become much more common, and the number of spells represented increases greatly.

The spells of the *Book of the Dead* cover a wide variety of topics, mainly designed to provide the deceased with the information and magical powers needed for his

transition to a state of eternal blessedness. Some deal with the dangerous period between death and the funeral itself, and outline the rituals to be performed at the tomb. Others pay homage to, or identify the deceased with, particular gods. Certain spells relate to the association of the deceased with the sun god, as one of the blessed dead who could travel with Re in his day- and night-time barks. Others deal with amulets, detailing their colors and where they should be placed on the mummy for the protection of the deceased on his perilous journey to the next world.

Weighing of the Heart and the Fields of Iaru

One of the single most important chapters of the *Book of the Dead* is 125 (according to a modern numbering system), the Weighing of the Heart. This represents the culmination of the deceased's journey to the Netherworld. After passing many obstacles, he was imagined to reach the Hall of Judgment. Led by the falcon-headed Horus, he was brought to face Osiris, often accompanied by Isis and Nephthys, in the presence of 42 gods. The deceased addresses each of these gods in turn, naming them and stating that he has done no wrong in his life: "O Embracer of Fire, who comes forth from Kher-Aha: I have not done violent robbery"; or "O Overthrower, who comes forth from Canopus: I have not trespassed."

After this "Negative Confession," Horus would take the deceased's heart and hand it to the jackal-headed god Anubis to weigh on a scale against the ostrich plume that represented *ma'at*, loosely translatable as justice and truth. The result was recorded by ibis-headed Thoth. If the pans balanced, the deceased would be welcomed by Osiris and the other gods into the company of the blessed dead, and could move on to eternal existence in the Fields of Iaru. If the scale did not balance, the heart would be fed to a monstrous creature named Ammit, and the unworthy deceased would be thrown into the lake of fire to die a second time, this time forever. Once the deceased had passed the test of the Weighing of the Heart, he or she could proceed to an eternal life in the Fields of Iaru (Reeds), or the Fields of the Blessed. Here, forever in the prime of life, they would enjoy an idyllic existence, surrounded by abundant food and drink, free of all cares and responsibilities.

Playing Senet

The boardgame *Senet* was a popular pastime, known as early as the 3rd Dynasty, in which opponents threw gaming sticks to guide the moves of their pieces around a board with 30 squares. By the end of the 18th Dynasty, this was evolving into a highly symbolic game, in which the deceased could play against an invisible opponent (perhaps his soul), in order to reach the afterlife safely. From this time on, gameboards have images and inscriptions in their squares that transform them into miniature models of the Netherworld, with the squares representing important locations and events from the Netherworld Books.

THE BOOKS OF THE UNDERWORLD

The *Book of the Amduat*, *Book of Gates*, *Book of the Earth* and *Book of Caverns* all focus on the journey of the sun god through the Netherworld during the 12 hours of the night. In contrast to the *Book of the Dead*, which is an illustrated

The sacred cat of Heliopolis (the center of the sun cult) slays the evil serpent Apophis under the *ished* tree, in this scene from the tomb of the royal artisan Inerkhau (TT 359).

collection of spells, these books are highly annotated depictions of the landscape and inhabitants of the Netherworld itself. The sun god was imagined to grow old during the day and then die at dusk and descend to the Netherworld. There he is shown, accompanied by various other gods and the blessed dead, traveling in his bark along the waterway of the Netherworld, which was seen as an otherwordly mirror image of the Nile. Along the way he and his company faced numerous dangers, most potent of which was the great serpent Apophis (or Apep).

At the midpoint of the journey (in the depth of the night), the sun god reached the furthest reaches of the Netherworld, the great caverns, or in other versions the Hall of Judgment, where he would meet and join with Osiris. The magical power generated by this union, which also symbolized the rejoining of the *ba* (sun god) and mummified body (Osiris), enabled the revitalized sun god to continue through the remainder of the night and to be reborn the next dawn, and thus to begin the cycle again. In the *Book of Gates*, the hours are divided by massive doors, each guarded by a huge snake. The deceased was required to know the name of the snakes, and the proper spells to utter, in order to pass these safely.

These books are at first depicted only on the walls of royal tombs. The images and texts provided the deceased king with the information he needed to succeed in his perilous quest for immortality, including the names of the demons and demigods he would encounter and the proper identification of the gates and other obstacles he would have to pass, along with the utterances that should ideally be made at each stage of the journey. Several of the Theban tombs include scenes and texts from these books, generally placed in the burial chambers, in a clear usurpation of royal privilege. A number of them date to the 18th Dynasty, including that of Useramun (TT 131 and TT 61), Vizier under Thutmose III, who decorated the walls of his burial chamber with texts from the *Book of Amduat*. His steward, Amememhat (TT 82), adorned his burial chamber with texts from the *Book of the Dead*, as well as excerpts from the Pyramid Texts. A number of Theban tombs, especially those at Deir el-Medina, contain images taken from the *Book of Gates*, though the *Book of the Earth* and the *Book of Caverns* are also represented.

LEFT
On the ceiling of the Ramesside tomb of Khonsumes (TT 30), Scribe of the Treasury in the Estate of Amun-Re, are two back-to-back images: one shows Re journeying in his boat adored by baboons and jackals, and the other depicts the tomb owner himself, worshipping Re-Horakhty.

PAGES 208–09
The ceiling of Sennedjem's tomb (TT 1) is adorned with many wonderful scenes, including this image of the falcon-headed sun god, Re-Horakhty, traveling across the sky in his bark accompanied by the sacred *benu* bird (the Greek phoenix), and the Ennead (nine gods).

The painted false door in the tomb of Huy, a sculptor of the god Amun (TT 54), is colored pink to resemble granite; the "door" is surrounded by scenes of offerings and cult rituals.

CHAPTER SIX

CULT RITUALS, OFFERING MEALS, AND BANQUETS

The culmination of the funeral was the performance of the cult itself. This took place first at the time of the burial, and was then in theory repeated for perpetuity. Fundamental to the celebration of this cult was the offering meal, in which the deceased was offered food and drink. It was through this cult, consisting of the ongoing performance of rites and the presentation of offerings, that the tomb owner and his family would be transformed and sustained for eternity.

Ideally, the cult would be performed by a relative and/or priest playing the role of the eldest son as Horus to the deceased's Osiris. However, the Egyptians were pragmatic, and knew that at some point there would probably be no one left to carry out their cults. Images of the tomb owner, often accompanied by his wife or other members of his immediate family, receiving offerings and as the focus of rituals were thus an essential part of the tomb's decoration, guaranteeing that the cult would magically continue forever. Cult images can appear multiple times within the same tomb, in a number of different locations. In fact, the tomb owner is generally represented in some way on each wall of the tomb. If he is facing out of the tomb (toward the ideal east, or away from the tomb's central axis), he is most likely receiving the cult in some way.

An extension of the representation of the funeral/cult meal was the banqueting scene, at which the tomb owner, his family, and assorted relatives and guests would enjoy food and drink and also often music and dancing. Such scenes are thought to represent both the actual meal that would have been eaten by the mourners after the burial was completed, and also annual celebrations such as the Beautiful Feast of the Valley, when relatives and friends would come to the necropolis to commune with the blessed dead.

FALSE DOORS AND CULT STATUES

The ultimate focus of the cult in the Theban tombs was usually either a false door or a statue niche. The false door was one of the earliest features of the elite tomb. Originally consisting of a simple niche in the west wall of the chapel into which was set a stela carved with an image of the tomb owner seated before an offering table, this was an essential element of the upper chapel, as it provided magical access to the burial chamber below. The *ka* of the deceased was imagined to emerge from the mummy where it was housed, ascend the burial shaft, and appear through this niche to partake of the offerings and benefit from cult rituals. The *ba* could also use this mystical portal to leave the tomb and wander the earth.

Over time, this niche with its small stela developed into an elaborate model door, generally made of stone but sometimes of wood, complete with jambs, a lintel, and a more or less complex sequence of niches. In the center was a "doorway," with the image of a rolled up mat carved above to indicate that the door was open. The

A principal cult focus in the tomb chapel of Paser, Head Archer in the 18th Dynasty (TT 367), was this false door, painted to look as if it had been carved from granite, with texts picked out in blue. On either side of the door the chief cult celebrant, dressed in a leopard-skin robe and probably Paser's son, performs a variety of cult rituals for the deceased.

door was sometimes sculpted or painted to look as if it was covered with textiles, and the lintels and jambs were generally adorned with the names and titles of the deceased, along with offering prayers. The traditional form for such prayers begins with the words *hetep di nesu*, "an offering which the king gives," and continues by asking that rituals be performed and food and drink offered, usually through the intercession of a god such as Osiris or Anubis. Above the central niche was often set the slab stela, decorated with an image of the tomb owner before a table of offerings.

Granite was an expensive stone for the ancient Egyptians, and some limestone doors were painted pink to make them appear as if they were carved from this desirable material. In the New Kingdom Theban tombs, many "false doors" are simply painted onto the flat wall and colored to resemble granite. The false doors in these tombs are most often found either at the back of the tomb or on the ideal south wall of the first chamber.

In many tomb chapels, the cult focus consisted of a three-dimensional image of the tomb owner, together with selected members of his family, that was placed or carved in the back (ideal west) chamber or niche of the chapel. Sometimes these were free-standing statues, but few have been found *in situ* in modern times, since they were looted long ago. However, many of the cult images were carved from the living rock in a tradition that dates back to at least the Middle Kingdom. These may derive in turn from certain Old Kingdom false doors that contained life-sized figures of the deceased's *ka* stepping out of the central niche. Like the painted and relief-carved walls, the statues were roughly cut from the poor quality rock of the hillsides into which the tombs were built, then enhanced with plaster and finally painted in vivid colors. Free-standing statues were carved from better quality limestone, but were also plastered and painted.

Seated statues of First Royal Herald, Duaneheh, and members of his family, form the cult focus in his tomb (TT 125). These were carved from the rock and then plastered and painted.

This statue of the Ramesside treasury official and scribe Nefersekheru in his festival finery stands in a niche at the back of his tomb (TT 296).

Whenever the offering cult was celebrated, the *ka* was believed to ascend from the burial chamber and rise through the burial shaft to take up temporary residence within these statues. The walls near these central images would be decorated with images of the cult rituals, especially the offering meal (see below).

CULT RITUALS

Precisely performed rituals were an essential part of Egyptian religion. Believed to invoke magical powers, such ceremonies involved spoken words accompanied by gestures and the proper use of amulets and cult objects. The rites of the mortuary cult echoed the elaborate series of rituals that were carried out to feed and care for the gods in their divine temples. These began at dawn, when the purified king or his delegate would awaken the god's image within its sanctuary, wash, anoint, and dress it, and burn incense to open the interface between the divine and earthly realms and bring the image to life. Meals, including meat, bread, fruit, and vegetables, were offered over the course of the day (and then redistributed to temple staff); at dusk the statue would be put to sleep and the sanctuary sealed for the night. On special occasions, the divine image would emerge from its inner shrine and travel – most often hidden from view inside a cult bark – either within the temple precinct or to related temples, when the god would visit other divinities.

The mortuary cult carried out for private people would have been similar, but less elaborate and less frequently performed. In addition, as well as caring for and feeding the *ka*, or life-force, of the tomb owner, mortuary rites served to ensure his eternal resurrection. This transformation took place first as the culmination of the funeral ceremony, and was then repeated at regular intervals, echoing the daily cycle of the sun.

THE OFFERING MEAL

The icon of the deceased seated in front of a table piled high with offerings is one of the oldest images in Egyptian art. By the Old Kingdom, it had reached the standard form in which it continued, albeit with variations and additions, for the remainder of pharaonic history. The fundamental elements are the tomb owner himself, in many cases accompanied by his wife, but in some cases other members of his immediate family, seated on a chair with an offering table before him. It is clear from the accompanying inscriptions that the cult recipients have already

The Mayor of the Southern City, Sennefer (TT 96), holds a lotus blossom to his nose, as his wife Meryt offers him strips of pure white linen, essential items for the burial and cult.

Suenmut, Royal Butler Clean of Hands (TT 92), sits in front of cult offerings for his eternal sustenance, forming a great tower of foodstuffs including bread, cuts of meat, fowl, and baskets containing a variety of fruits.

undergone the necessary rituals by which they have become blessed spirits, able to eat and drink in the afterlife. The eldest son ideally officiates at the offering meal, as he does at the other rituals.

Primary locations for offering scenes were in the cult niche or chamber at the back of the tomb, one of the focal walls opposite the entrance in the first hall, or in association with the false door, which was most often found in the first hall, on the ideal south wall, and cult statues. In New Kingdom Theban tombs, the tomb owner is generally shown seated on a chair with a high back and feline legs; his wife, who is depicted behind him according to the principles of Egyptian perspective, but who would in reality have been beside him, usually has her own, similar chair. In some examples, the tomb owner and his wife sit together on a couch or bed. This is thought to have erotic connotations and also to imbue the scene with overtones of fertility and rebirth. These implications can be reinforced by the addition underneath the couch of erotically charged objects such as mirrors or cosmetic and perfume vessels. Depictions of dogs and cats under the chairs suggested male virility and female fertility respectively. These aspects were essential both for the continuation of the pleasures of life in the hereafter, and, perhaps more importantly, to help ensure the eternal rebirth of the deceased through the sexual union. The chair sits on a reed mat, and inscriptions sometimes inform us that the entire scene is meant to take place within a "booth," which can be interpreted as the tomb itself.

Many different costumes are worn by the cult recipients in these scenes. Both husband and wife might have floral collars tied around their necks. These, made

primarily of the petals of the white and blue lotus, were known as *wah* collars, and have been shown to symbolize rebirth and regeneration, as well as to help guarantee the eternal provisioning of the cult. Such collars were worn by the members of the funeral party and at subsequent celebrations of the Beautiful Feast of the Valley; they were also draped around the necks of the anthropoid coffins and statues of the deceased. Another type of necklace often seen was the *weskhet*, or broad collar, usually made of beads in imitation of floral motifs. These were also worn on festival occasions, and had overtones of protection.

The cult recipients can be depicted with unguent cones – funnel-shaped blocks of scented wax – set on their heads. Some scholars have suggested that these cones were not actually worn in real life, but are shown simply to indicate that the person is wearing perfume. If they were worn in reality, they would presumably have been made of beeswax or ox tallow scented with myrrh, and would have imparted a pleasant odor to the wearer. It is argued that such cones would have served a practical purpose, not only keeping the wearer smelling fresh even in the heat of summer, but also permeating the hair and clothes with perfume, conveying overtones of eroticism and thus rebirth.

The tomb owner might also hold or wear items related to his earthly status, such as a staff of office; a *shebyu* collar, awarded as a mark of distinction; or a handkerchief, an important symbol of status and rank. Wives can be shown holding sistra (sacred rattles), connecting them with their roles as priestesses of Hathor.

A line of cult celebrants carrying ceramic vessels and garlands, led by the son of the deceased, approach a figure (not visible here) of Ptah-Sokar-Osiris, in the Ramesside tomb chapel (TT 341) of the Chief of the Altar in the Ramesseum (the mortuary temple of Ramesses II), Nakhtamun. At the end of the procession are two seated musicians.

PAGES 218–19
These beautifully carved offering bearers carry abundant foodstuffs to replenish the cult and ensure that the tomb owner, the vizier Ramose, will be provided with all necessities for eternity (TT 55).

In front of the tomb owner and his wife is usually a table or reed mat heaped high with a variety of foodstuffs. There would be bread, vegetables, such as onions and leeks (or sometimes lettuce, strongly linked with fertility), fruit, choice cuts of meat, and prepared fowl. In some cases, fish, earlier excluded from such scenes, might be included. Also seen here might be a bouquet of lotus blossoms, a symbol of resurrection referred to in texts as a "life" bouquet and generally associated with Amun-Re or Hathor. During the Beautiful Feast of the Valley, such bouquets were placed around the shrine of Hathor at Deir el-Bahari as offerings to Amun, and would later have been distributed to the private cults.

Flanking the reed mat piled with food are often vessels full of water, milk, beer, or wine; and vases filled with unguents and perfumes. Although shown above and below the mat, according to the principles of Egyptian art, these would in reality have been placed on either side of it. Water, milk, and beer were basic staples of the Egyptian diet, and wine could produce an altered state of consciousness, bringing the realms of the human and divine closer together.

To ensure that the deceased was provided with all necessary food, drink, and other essentials, the depictions of offerings piled on and around the table could be supplemented with a hieroglyphic list of food and other necessities for the afterlife, along with instructions, arranged in a grid. The *sem* priest was responsible for magically activating this list, so that its contents would be eternally available to the cult recipients.

PAGES 220–22
This double image occupies the back wall of the tomb chapel of Amenemhat (TT 340), a Servant in the Place of Truth in the early 18th Dynasty. To the left of the central niche, above which is painted a row of vessels, are Amenemhat's parents; to the right, the deceased and his wife, Reditiah, also sit before a table piled high with offerings. Beneath both women's chairs stand a mirror and a cosmetics vessel.

Men and women enjoying a banquet, in the 18th Dynasty tomb of Djehuty, Steward of the High Priest of Amun (TT 45), which was usurped in the 19th Dynasty by Djehutyemheb, Head of the Makers of Fine Linen of the Estate of Amun. On the left, the wife and daughter of the deceased offer cult items to a goddess. The seated female guests have perfume cones on their heads and are attended by servant girls who pour unguents over their hands and offer them flowers and jewelry. Rows of large jars, beautifully painted to represent their material and decoration, occupy the center.

Servants slaughter a cow and carry in the head and leg of the animal, as its blood is collected in a bowl, in the tomb of Pekhsukher Tjenenu (TT 88). The foreleg was regarded as the choicest cut and is often seen amongst the great piles of food depicted on offering tables.

PAGES 227–28
One of the most elegant banqueting scenes in the Theban repertoire comes from the tomb of Ramose (TT 55). Seen here in the prime of their youth are the unfinished figures of Ramose's friends and relatives, the couples seated side by side so that they can enjoy this festive celebration together for eternity.

An important element of tomb decoration from the Old Kingdom onward are files of servants bringing offerings to replenish the cult. All varieties of foodstuffs and drinks are represented in these scenes, which generally cover many registers and can include numerous bearers. In addition to prepared food, the servants bring live animals, including cattle, to be slaughtered, flocks of fowl, and desert animals caught in the hunt.

BANQUETING

A complement to the offering meal is the banqueting scene, which includes the deceased and his immediate and extended family (both living and dead), friends, and professional colleagues. A number of scholars have studied these scenes in depth, and have concluded that they represent an eternal celebration of the funerary meal (attended by friends and relatives) and its later re-enactments, such as the feasts that were held during the annual Beautiful Feast of the Valley. The tomb owner and his family may also have enjoyed such feasts before death, perhaps even in the courtyard or inside the tomb itself. Such banqueting scenes contain complex symbolism: through the link with the funerary meal they connect the guests with Osiris, while in their evocation of the Beautiful Feast of the Valley they associate them with Amun and Hathor. They are also full of imagery that evokes fertility and eroticism, thus contributing to the eternal rebirth and resurrection of the deceased; and in their representation of food and drink, they help to ensure the perpetual provisioning of the cult.

The guests, eternally in their prime and dressed in their holiday best, with unguent cones on their heads, are seated on chairs, stools, or on reed mats on the floor. Sometimes the men and women are shown separately, but married couples can also be together, either side-by-side on individual chairs, or on couches. The tomb owner and his wife occupy the place of honor.

Food is placed in dishes below the chairs of the banqueters, or heaped on tables in front of each register of guests. Servants offer cups of wine and jars of beer, so that the participants can drink to excess, helping to break down the barriers between the earthly and divine realms. Guests often hold a lotus blossom to their noses. As a symbol, this had overtones of eroticism and thus rebirth; in practical terms, certain types of lotuses were also known for their narcotic properties, and may have been used to produce altered states of consciousness. Mandrake plants, which have hallucinogenic properties and were considered aphrodisiacs, are also seen at these banquets.

Servants are shown tending to the guests' wigs or unguent cones, or adorning them with elaborate collars. Female servants are often all but naked, wearing only jewelry and a girdle that leaves their breasts and pubic areas exposed, creating a clearly erotic ambience.

MUSIC AND DANCING

Music and dance were important elements of the successful banquet, not only giving great pleasure to the guests but also helping them reach the altered states of consciousness that brought them closer to the blessed dead. Musicians and dancers were connected with Hathor, goddess of the sky, love, and motherhood. Hathoric rites, generally performed by women, usually featured the sistrum, a sacred rattle whose sound mimicked the noise of the wind rustling through the papyrus plants that grew in the Delta marshes. These marshes were themselves closely associated with the creation of the universe and with the birth of the god Horus. Sistra were also used in connection with other divine cults during this era, such as that of the feline goddess Bastet.

Much of Egyptian secular and religious life was marked by the performance of music and dance. Ceremonial palettes and stone vessels dating as far back as the Predynastic era indicate the prominent role that music played even in the earliest periods of Egyptian history. The importance of music in daily life in ancient Egypt is underscored by the large number of pharaonic musical instruments found today in museum collections around the world.

In banqueting scenes, the instruments depicted most often were the flute, lute, harp, and pipes, with hand cymbals and tambourines used for rhythm. Novel instruments in the New Kingdom included the seven-stringed harp, long-necked lute, and double flute, played vertically, more like a modern oboe or clarinet. In addition to instrumentalists, many tombs contain singers. The voice was thought to bring life and health to the gods, and by extension to the deceased. In some

The banqueting scene in the mid-18th Dynasty tomb of Nakht, Scribe and Astronomer of Amun (TT 52), features the icon of the blind harper entertaining the guests.

Also from the tomb of Nakht comes this well-known image of a troupe of three beautiful female musicians, one playing a double flute, one with a small lute, and the third with a harp. Music was an important element of the banquet.

tombs, the words of the songs are included in these scenes, and show clearly that they were closely connected to the cult.

Dance was both a sport and a religious ritual for the ancient Egyptians. Pharaonic dance was a combination of graceful movements and acrobatics, and required great strength and flexibility. It was often performed in pairs or groups, and props such as balls and staffs could be used. In the New Kingdom, professional dancers were trained in special schools, which are shown in the tomb of Ay at Amarna as a separate building next to the palace.

The painted and carved scenes that covered the walls of the tombs of the nobles at Thebes were an essential element in the successful transition of the deceased to the eternal afterlife, but the tomb owners also needed certain specific items of equipment to be buried with them, and these are the subject of the next chapter.

Untiring workers for eternity, these shabti figures, shown against a backdrop of the striped boxes in which they were found, come from the tomb of royal grandparents Yuya and Tjuya (KV 46).

CHAPTER SEVEN

TAKING IT WITH YOU: BURIAL EQUIPMENT

Imagine if most of the Theban tombs had been found intact! We would have treasures beyond compare, giving us enormous insight into the world of pharaonic Egypt. When I visit these tombs, found empty and stripped of their funerary equipment, two things come to my mind. First, I wonder what we would have learned if even half of these tombs had been discovered inviolate. And then I imagine the ancient thieves – how they might have schemed with each other and planned their robberies. Perhaps there were two men living on the East Bank of the Nile, who would swim in secret across the river and hide from the necropolis police until they could enter the tombs, plundering them of their gold, precious oils, and jewels – everything valuable they could carry.

Fortunately, several New Kingdom private tombs have been discovered with their burial chambers (where the mummies and their equipment were stored) still filled with their original furnishings. These fabulous artifacts, together with additional objects left behind in various tombs by ancient or modern robbers, or looted long ago and now in museums around the world, provide us with a wealth of information both about how the ancient Egyptians conceived of life after death and what they considered necessary to take with them to the afterlife.

THE GREAT DISCOVERIES

The thrill of discovery is something that most people do not have the chance to experience, and there are few published accounts that convey the feelings of an archaeologist who makes a great find. I am one of the fortunate people who have made exciting new discoveries. The occasions when I uncover something that has not been seen by human eyes for millennia are truly the greatest moments in my life. One of my first big finds was the tomb of an Old Kingdom dwarf named Perniankhu, whose job was to dance for the king. Inside the burial shaft was the skeleton of the dwarf himself, and in a walled-up chamber above was a beautiful statue showing him seated on a chair. I will never forget the moment when I held this statue in my arms for the first time. Much more recently, I entered the mysterious tunnel leading from the burial chamber of the tomb of Seti I, which we are currently excavating, as mentioned in the introduction. Exploring this narrow, rocky shaft that leads deep into the Theban cliffs, not knowing where it will lead us, is a wonderful experience. One day when I was inside this tunnel, a large stone fell on my toe. I felt pain, and saw blood; later I learned that I had broken my toe. This sort of adventure is not without its dangers! But the hazards that we face are part of the thrill, and make the final discovery even sweeter.

The years from the late 19th into the early 20th centuries were filled with great discoveries in Egyptology. Featured in this chapter will be four of these discoveries, all Theban tombs of the New Kingdom, which illustrate the sorts of fabulous artifacts noble burials once contained. From the Valley of the Kings come two non-royal burials: the 18th Dynasty tomb of the courtier Maiherpri and the burial of royal in-laws Yuya and Tjuya; and from Deir el-Medina come the 18th Dynasty tomb of an important official, Kha, and the 19th Dynasty tomb of the artisan Sennedjem.

MAIHERPRI (KV 36)

The tomb of Maiherpri was excavated in 1899 by Victor Loret, then head of the Egyptian Antiquities Service. The burial, which lies in the Valley of the Kings, consists of a small, undecorated chamber near the great tomb of Amenhotep II (KV 35), which had been discovered by Loret the year before. The story of the find has never been fully published, but we know that it was almost completely intact and contained many wonderful things, including the mummy of Maiherpri himself.

Maiherpri ("lion on the battlefield") bore the titles Child of the Royal Nursery, indicating that he was raised and educated in the palace, and Royal Fanbearer, showing that he was a member of the king's bodyguard. He is certain to have grown up with one of the great pharaohs of the 18th Dynasty, most likely either Amenhotep II or Thutmose IV. The fact that he was awarded burial in the Valley of the Kings confirms that he had a close personal relationship with the king. In my recent work in the Valley of the Kings we have found a graffito that says, "Userhat built a tomb for his father, the vizier Amennakht," which shows that non-royal people buried in the royal necropolis were generally very important, with high titles or close connections to the royal house.

Maiherpri's mummy, as well as his image on the spectacular copy of the *Book of the Dead* (*Book of Coming Forth by Day*) with which he was buried, shows that he had Nubian blood. We know that the Egyptians insisted that foreign chieftains and vassals send their sons to be brought up at the Egyptian court, in order to ensure their loyalty, and it is possible that Maiherpri was a Nubian prince. It is equally possible that he was the scion of a Nubian family that had long been living in Egypt. He died young, around the age of 24. His expertise as an archer is borne out by the artifacts found with him in his tomb, including a quiver and arrows. Depictions of desert hunts usually show the hunters accompanied by dogs, and two dog collars were buried with Maiherpri.

OPPOSITE

Above: A number of pottery vessels once containing precious oils and unguents, as well as other materials, were found in Maiherpri's tomb, along with items from his life as a hunter, such as this dog collar. Other equipment in the tomb included a quiver and arrows.

Below: Painted black and adorned with figures and hieroglyphs in gold, this wooden shrine held Maiherpri's canopic material – his separately mummified lungs, liver, stomach, and intestines. Visible on the end are the protective goddesses Isis and Nephthys, and on the side the canopic genii Imsety and Hapy, here both shown as human-headed.

Maiherpri, his skin color reflecting his Nubian ancestry, raises his arms in worship before the god Osiris in a vignette from his 2¼-meter long funerary papyrus.

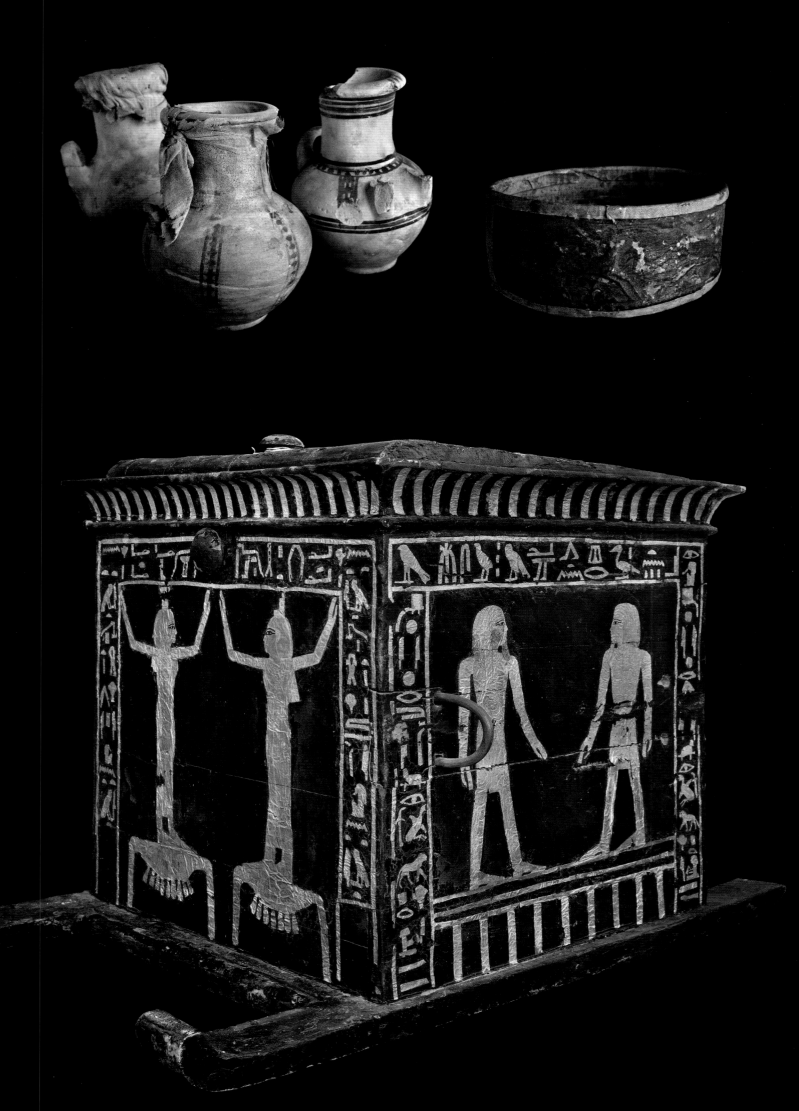

YUYA AND TJUYA (KV 46)

One of the most fascinating and powerful queens of Egypt's Golden Age was Tiye, chief consort of Amenhotep III. Her image features prominently in the royal art of her husband's reign, and her importance is underscored by a series of scarabs issued in his 11th year, which appear to announce their marriage. The inscription on these scarabs gives the pharaoh's names and epithets, and then names the "Great Royal Wife, Tiye." It also tells us the name of her father, Yuya, and her mother, Tjuya. Often said to have been of "common" birth, it is clear now that Tiye's parents were members of an important noble family from Akhmim in Middle Egypt, and most likely wielded a great deal of political power before the marriage of their daughter to the king. Yuya bore a number of military titles: Royal Lieutenant Commander of Chariotry and Master of the Horse, as well as Priest of Min. Tjuya was Chantress of Hathor, Chantress of Amun, and Chief of the Entertainers of both Amun and Min – all major religious titles.

As a consequence of their daughter's status, Yuya and Tjuya were greatly honored with burial in the Valley of the Kings. Only their tomb chamber is in the royal burial ground; their above-ground chapel has never been identified, but would probably have been located either in the Valley of the Nobles, near the other late 18th Dynasty chapels, or near Amenhotep III's mortuary temple at the edge of the low desert.

In the early 20th century, the concession to dig in the Valley of the Kings was held by an American businessman named Theodore Davis. Beginning in 1902, the archaeologist who carried out the actual excavations for him was Howard Carter, later made famous by the discovery of the tomb of Tutankhamun. In 1904, Englishman James Quibell took Carter's place. Quibell concentrated his work in the area between KV 3, the tomb of the sons of Ramesses III, and KV 4, the tomb of Ramesses XI. On 6 February 1905, his workmen found the top of a staircase cut into the valley floor, beneath a pile of debris almost 10 meters high.

Quibell, who had earlier requested a transfer, left the site the next day to act as tour guide for the Duke of Connaught. It was thus Arthur Weigall, who had been tentatively appointed as Quibell's replacement, who supervised the clearing of the staircase. Five days later, just as night was falling, he and his workmen discovered a doorway, still mostly blocked with limestone that had been covered with mud plaster and stamped with the necropolis seal: a jackal over nine captives. An opening at the top of the blocking told the excavators that thieves had beaten them into the tomb. Weigall and the *reis* (the Egyptian head of the workmen) spent the night guarding the tomb.

Davis was relaxing in his *dahabiya* (houseboat) when the doorway was uncovered, and he did not come to see the great discovery until late the next day. When he arrived, he and Weigall tried to peer into the corridor beyond, but could see little. Rather than take the time to fetch a ladder so they could enter themselves, they lifted up one of the basket boys (apparently the son of the *reis*) so that he could slip through the small opening, using a head wrap to lower him to the floor of the corridor beyond. The boy was frightened at first, but then collected several objects that lay on the corridor floor (including a wooden staff, a chariot yoke, and a gold-covered scarab), which he handed back to the waiting archaeologists.

Gaston Maspero, then Head of the Antiquities Service, was in Luxor at the time, also on his *dahabiya*. Davis brought the objects to him, and the two returned to the Valley of the Kings together the next day. There are various versions of what happened next (as is usual for major discoveries!), but all agree that events moved very quickly. Beyond the blocking was a descending corridor that led to a second steep flight of stairs, at the bottom of which was another blocked doorway, again open at the top. According to Davis, he, Weigall, and Maspero were the first to enter the burial chamber, where the light from their candles picked up the glitter of

The outer anthropoid coffin of Yuya is disproportionately large, in order to hold the two nested inner coffins that in turn contained the mummy.

OPPOSITE
Several items of beautiful furniture, clearly from the royal workshops, were found in the tomb of Yuya and Tjuya. The back of this gilded wooden chair bears a scene showing their daughter, Tiye, Great Royal Wife of Amenhotep III, seated on a chair in a papyrus boat, accompanied by two of her own daughters.

Standing on lion's paws, this bed from the tomb of Yuya and Tjuya was carved from wood and strung with linen twine. The headboard is adorned with three panels containing figures of the protective household deities Bes (a dwarf with the head and tail of a lion) and Tawaret (a composite of hippopotamus, lion, and crocodile).

A view into the tomb of Kha (TT 8) at the time of its discovery in 1906, giving some indication of what the tombs of the nobles would once have contained – and what has been lost. Around the edges are pieces of furniture draped in cloths, and in the mass of objects in the middle are numerous vessels containing a variety of foodstuffs.

gold. Although ancient robbers had violated the tomb at least once, what remained was still extraordinary: coffins; chests; beds; chairs; pottery jars filled with natron (used in mummification); boxes filled with dried foodstuffs; a wig and wig basket; and even a small chariot. The tomb was a mess – the objects had been thrown about, most of the jewelry had been stolen, and the coffins had been opened and the mummies ransacked. But the many treasures left behind made this tomb the greatest discovery in the Valley of the Kings before Tutankhamun.

When Quibell returned, he was shocked to find that Davis had removed objects without proper documentation or preservation. He threw himself into the systematic clearance of the tomb, and, at Maspero's command, recorded and removed all the objects within three weeks. The funerary assemblage of Yuya and Tjuya now forms one of the central collections of the Egyptian Museum, Cairo.

During the writing of this book, I had the opportunity to examine the mummies of Yuya and Tjuya as part of my project to research the family of Tutankhamun. As the mother and father of Queen Tiye, these nobles would probably have been the great-grandparents of the boy-king. We carried out CT-scans of both mummies, and took samples for DNA analysis. We hope that our research can help us identify the mummy of Tiye, and clarify Tutankhamun's parentage.

KHA (TT 8)

Only a year after the discovery of Yuya and Tjuya, the Italian archaeologist Ernesto Schiaparelli made his greatest find. Schiaparelli had been working at Deir el-Medina since 1905, excavating on behalf of the Egyptian Museum, Turin. After weeks of work in the debris near the Ptolemaic Hathor Temple, he had uncovered very little. In the winter of 1905–06, he shifted his scene of operations to the village itself and the area on the western slopes of the nearby hills, close to a decorated chapel surmounted by a ruined mud-brick pyramid. This chapel had been discovered in the early 19th century by Bernardino Drovetti, who had removed a painted stela belonging to a couple named Kha and Meryt. There was no burial chamber beneath the chapel, but the Italians hoped it might be nearby. After almost a month of work, Schiaparelli and his team of 250 workmen exposed a roughly cut

triangle in the cliff face that had been sealed with stone debris; when this was cleared, a set of steep stairs was exposed. At the bottom of these stairs was a wall of stone and mortar, apparently still intact. Schiaparelli made a small breach in the wall, and asked his *reis*, Khalifa, to squeeze through. Moments later, Reis Khalifa emerged, yelling with excitement. The tomb was intact! A second sealed door lay behind the first.

Two of the Italian team kept watch over the tomb all night, and the next day Arthur Weigall arrived to supervise the opening of the tomb. Beyond the blocking wall was a horizontal corridor, at the end of which lay another wall, this time of dry stone. When this second wall was dismantled, the archaeologists found themselves in the tomb's antechamber, in which several artifacts, including a wooden standing lamp, several baskets, a small wooden latrine, and a low bed, had been stored. This was apparently the overflow from the burial chamber itself. At the far end was a simple wooden door closed with a wooden locking device. It looked brand-new, and Schiaparelli even jokingly asked one of his servants to find him the key!

When the team breached the sealed door (by removing one of the panels), they found the burial intact, undisturbed for over 3,000 years. The final chamber was rectangular and had a vaulted ceiling. It had been built for a Chief of the Great Place named Kha, whose career spanned the reigns of Amenhotep II, Thutmose IV, and Amenhotep III. Kha and his wife, Meryt, were buried with wonderful funerary equipment, including their coffins, two shabtis (see p. 245), a beautiful *ka* statuette, linens, a cabinet containing a woman's wig, a bronze lamp, various toilet and cosmetic items, clothing, and storage vessels of pottery and stone. Most amazing perhaps were the tables, some laden with bread and cakes, others holding vessels containing a wide variety of foodstuffs. The entire assemblage, save for one of the standing lamps, was taken to Italy, where it today forms one of the principal collections of the Egyptian Museum, Turin.

All the objects on this page were found in the intact tomb of Kha. The pottery vessels painted in bright colors may have contained liquids; the one on the right still has its cover, fastened with straps of linen. Among the items of furniture from the tomb were the folding stool and wooden linen chest seen below (left and center). The chest has a rather crudely painted funerary scene showing Kha and his wife Meryt seated before an offering table, attended to by their children. Below right is a model sarcophagus that contained one of Kha's shabtis.

SENNEDJEM (TT 1)

The earliest of the four tombs discussed here to be discovered (and the first Theban Tomb to be numbered) was the burial of Sennedjem. This great find took place in early 1886, during the annual tour of inspection taken by Gaston Maspero. By the end of January, Maspero and the other members of his scientific expedition had arrived in Luxor. On the evening of 1 February, a villager from Qurna named Salam Abu Duhi came to tell them that, after only seven days of officially approved excavations, he and three friends had uncovered an intact tomb at Deir el-Medina. The burial chamber had been covered by debris from other tombs, and had thus escaped previous notice. Maspero immediately sent a guard to watch over the tomb during the night, and the expedition set out at dawn the next day to examine the new discovery.

When they arrived, they found that there was no above-ground structure remaining to mark the location of the tomb. At the bottom of a shaft cut about 4 meters deep into the living rock was an entrance that led to a narrow descending passage. This ended in a small undecorated chamber. A second shaft, about a meter deep, led to another passage that took the archaeologists to an entrance doorway, still closed with a wooden door, just as it had been left by the mortuary priests millennia before. The door, which was decorated with painted scenes, bore the name of the tomb owner, the Servant in the Place of Truth, Sennedjem.

After carefully removing the door for transport to the Boulaq Museum in Cairo (unfortunately by breaking the stone lintel above it), the team entered the burial chamber. Inside, they found nine coffins containing mummies, as well as 11 additional mummies simply lying on the floor. Around them were pottery vessels containing various foodstuffs, furniture, and dried flowers. The wall paintings were superbly preserved. However, the heat inside the tomb was unbearable, reaching 48 degrees centigrade.

Maspero's team, led by Spanish archaeologist Eduardo Toda, supervised the removal of the tomb's artifacts, to be taken by boat to Cairo. A certain number of artifacts, including what Toda described as a magnificent painted tabouret (a low stool), were destroyed during the removal process, and of the 11 uncoffined mummies, only the heads survived the trip.

The burial equipment of Sennedjem, alongside that of Maiherpri, now graces a gallery at the Egyptian Museum, Cairo.

The outer coffin of Sennedjem's son, Khonsu (from TT 1) is painted yellow, the color of divinity, and decorated with funerary texts, along with religious images often seen on tomb walls during the Ramesside era. The body inside was protected by the goddesses Serket and Neith (visible on the end), and Isis and Nephthys, along with other deities.

BURIAL EQUIPMENT

MUMMIES AND COFFINS

The central object necessary for any proper burial was, of course, the body of the deceased. Evidence of a desire to preserve the body in some form dates back to the earliest periods of Egyptian history. There are some indications that, from the late Predynastic era into the early Old Kingdom, the bodies of certain of the elite may have been allowed to decompose almost completely after death. Afterward, the disarticulated skeletons were reassembled and wrapped with linen to form simulacra of the deceased. Later, the Egyptians learned to desiccate the body, and thus prevent it from decaying, by washing it with wine, removing the water-filled viscera, then packing the corpse both inside and out with a type of salt called natron, so that all the liquid in the tissues would be leached out. The heart was generally left in the body, and the brain was removed and discarded. The resulting mummy was then anointed with perfumed oils and wrapped in linen, to create an eternal model of the deceased as a *sah* that could be reanimated to receive the resurrected spirit. Protective amulets were inserted into the wrappings at specific places, according to detailed instructions set out in texts such as the *Book of the Dead*.

During certain periods, the body and especially the face could also be modeled in plaster, or the face and other parts of the body could be echoed in wood, cartonnage (linen stiffened with plaster), or even metal, creating an idealized and everlasting effigy of the dead person. By the New Kingdom, most elite mummies were provided with funerary masks of cartonnage or gilded and painted wood. Funerary bands could be placed directly over the wrappings, copying the linen bands that held the outer bandages in place. The entire mummy, with mask and bands, was then deposited in an anthropoid coffin, most often made of stuccoed and painted wood. Like the mummy itself, this was, by the New Kingdom, in the form of the *sah*, or transformed body. For the wealthy, the first coffin was fitted inside a second, also anthropoid, and then the complete assemblage was placed into a rectangular outer sarcophagus, usually of wood. Many assemblages also include a "mummy board," a separate full-size figure of the deceased placed above the mummy, inside the innermost coffin.

These helmet-like masks made of gilded cartonnage were placed over the heads of the royal in-laws Tjuya (left) and Yuya (right). Both husband and wife wear long tripartite wigs and special necklaces known as *weskhet*, or broad collars; Tjuya's is inlaid with colored glass.

OPPOSITE
Once mummified, the body was placed within an anthropoid coffin. Above is the gilded wood inner (fourth) coffin of Yuya (KV 46); below is the painted wooden coffin of Sennedjem's wife, Isis (TT 1). Note that Isis is shown in the costume of daily life rather than mummy wrappings, a fashion that spanned the end of the 18th and the early 19th Dynasties.

Both coffins and sarcophagi were often decorated with images of protective deities, along with bands of inscription containing prayers and the name and titles of the deceased. On outer chests of the 18th Dynasty, the preference was for gilded and painted wood, with a black background against which gilded figures and bands were placed. In the late 18th Dynasty, a new type comes into use, with polychrome designs painted on a yellow or natural wood-colored background. In the late 18th and early 19th Dynasties, some coffins and mummy boards are carved to represent the deceased in the costume of everyday life, rather than in the mummy wrappings of the *sah*, but this type of coffin is only seen for a short time, and the elite went back to the traditional mummiform type. In general, the decoration of coffins becomes more elaborate over time, with figures filling more of the space.

CANOPIC MATERIAL

The viscera – specifically the stomach, lungs, intestines, and liver – were mummified separately and wrapped in four individual packages. These were then placed inside a "canopic" jar – ovoid vessels topped with stoppers that took the form of either human heads or the head of a jackal, a falcon, a baboon, and a man. Our modern name for these containers derives from a misidentification of the human-headed stoppers with the Hellenistic god Canopus, from the city of Canop near Alexandria, whose body took the shape of a jar. The four packages were each identified with one of the Four Sons of Horus (see p. 201): the stomach with jackal-headed Duamutef; the intestines with the falcon-headed Qebehsenuef; the lungs with the baboon-headed Hapy; and the liver with the human-headed Imsety (hence the forms of the stoppers). Each canopic genius was in turn protected by a

In the 18th Dynasty, most canopic jars were stoppered with human heads representing Imsety, Hapy, Qebehsenuef, and Duamutef, the Four Sons of Horus. Inside the set from which these two examples come were Tjuya's viscera, mummified and wrapped in bundles topped with small human-headed masks of gilded cartonnage.

RIGHT
The shabtis found in Yuya and Tjuya's tomb were of various sizes, and although other materials were used, most were made of wood, gilded and painted, and housed in boxes, like those shown here. They are inscribed with Spell 6 from the *Book of the Dead*, promising that if the tomb owner is called upon to work in the afterlife, the shabti will labor in his stead.

OPPOSITE
When it was discovered in 1886, the entrance to the burial chamber of Sennedjem (TT 1) was still closed with this wooden door, adorned with images of the tomb owner and his family worshipping Osiris and Ma'at (above) and the hawk-headed Ptah-Sokar-Osiris and Isis (below).

goddess: Neith, Serket, Nephthys, or Isis respectively. Like the coffins, the canopic jars might be placed inside nests of boxes and chests. Also like the coffins, the canopic chests were decorated with images of funerary deities such as Anubis, the jackal-headed god of embalming, the four canopic genii, or the four protective goddesses, arranged in vertical bands.

SHABTIS

Most New Kingdom burials also contained shabtis, funerary figurines that were placed in the tomb to work on behalf of the deceased in the afterlife, who would therefore not be doomed to eternal labor in the Fields of the Blessed. These small statuettes seem to have evolved from the Old Kingdom tradition of placing models of servants performing tasks such as grinding grain or brewing beer in tombs. In the late Old Kingdom, these single figures developed into elaborate models, with, for example, groups of butchers shown to scale within a slaughterhouse, or miniature scribes recording the amounts of grain placed in a dollhouse-sized granary.

Such models were only in use for a short time, and were replaced by figures representing the tomb owner himself, usually mummiform but in some cases wearing the clothing of daily life. Originally appearing during the First Intermediate Period, these figurines could be made of wax, stone, wood, faience, pottery, or sometimes glass.

During the 18th Dynasty, such figures became a standard part of the funerary assemblage, and were clearly identified as field laborers by the agricultural tools they often carried on their backs. Their number multiplied: by the reign of Tutankhamun, there could be over 400: one for each day of the year, an overseer for each 30-day month; and a supervisor for each 10-day week. Royal examples are made of various materials, but shabtis from private tombs are most often made of faience. Mid- to late New Kingdom examples are often inscribed with Chapter, or Spell, 6 from the *Book of the Dead*, in which the figure promises to answer should the deceased be called on to perform such tasks as cultivating fields, carrying out irrigation projects, or moving sand from one place to another. Shabtis (also known as shawabtis, and in later times ushabtis, "answerers") were stored in wooden boxes.

STATUARY

Although cult statues in Theban tombs were often cut into the living rock, some tombs contained free-standing statuary, either instead of the rock-cut images or in addition to them, although few of these have been found *in situ* in modern times. Such statues could vary in size and form: they could, for example, be simple statues of the tomb owner, standing or sitting, or could be naophorus statues, in which the

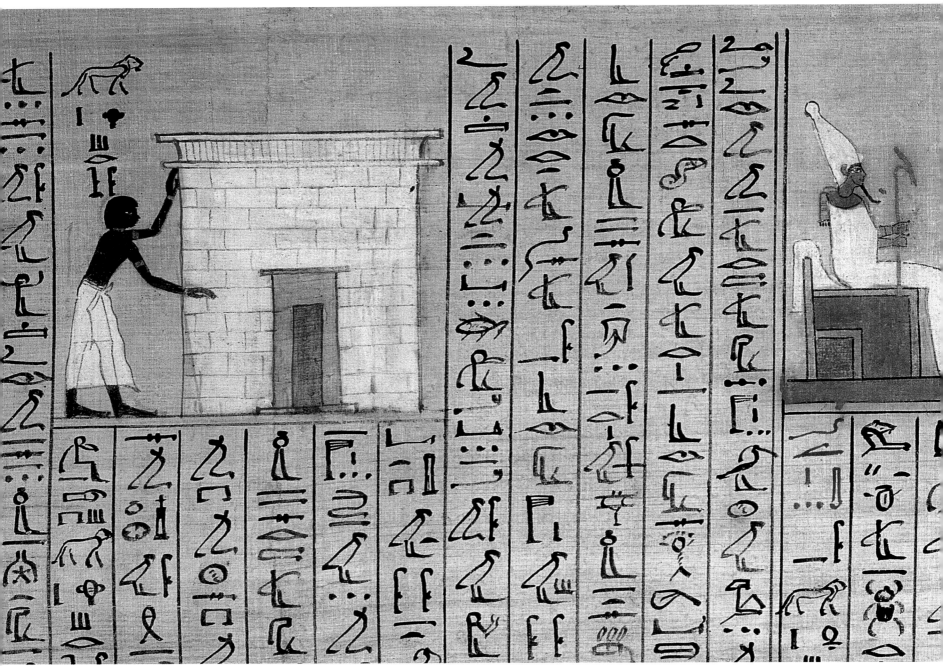

OPPOSITE
This unusual statuette represents Maiherpri's *ba*, an intangible aspect of the person that survived death and could leave the tomb to visit the world of the living. Shown with a head that is clearly meant to be Maiherpri himself, the figure has the body of a bird of prey.

Another section of Maiherpri's funerary papyrus (see also p. 234) depicts a version of the Weighing of the Heart ceremony, presided over by Osiris. On the right, Maiherpri's *ba* is shown leaving the tomb.

tomb owner kneels and offers a statue or stela. Statuary could come in other forms as well, although finds of non-human figures are rare outside the context of the royal tombs.

BOOK OF THE DEAD

An important item included in many New Kingdom burial assemblages was a copy of the *Book of the Dead* (see above, p. 201). Illustrated papyri containing texts and images from this important collection of funerary spells were placed in the tomb, generally in the burial chamber and sometimes with the mummy itself.

FOOD AND DRINK

Nourishment was essential for the afterlife. Pottery vessels containing various liquids, such as beer and wine, were included with burials, along with wooden boxes filled with different types of foods. The food found in Theban burials echoes the typical Egyptian diet, with bread and beer as the staple elements, supplemented by red meat, poultry, vegetables and fruits, and wine. Funerary food did not actually have to be edible – bread loaves could be of poor quality, and meat and fowl were often mummified.

The lid of this elegant chest of gilded wood and faience is embellished with the cartouches of Amenhotep III, son-in-law of the tomb's owners, Yuya and Tjuya. This royal connection may be the reason why they were honored with burial in the Valley of the Kings.

Yuya was an important army officer – one of his titles was Royal Lieutenant Commander of Chariotry – and he was buried with this splendid chariot. The Egyptian chariot was designed to carry two people, but was lightweight so that it could maneuver easily.

FURNITURE, CLOTHING, AND COSMETICS

Wealthy Egyptians owned a certain amount of furniture, and they took this with them to the tomb for use in the afterlife. Such items included chairs, beds, and chests and cabinets for the storage of jewelry and clothing. A number of wigs have been found in funerary contexts, and various items of clothing have been discovered. Toilet articles such as unguent jars in various sizes, kohl tubes (containing eye makeup) and applicators, razors, combs, and tweezers were considered essential for the afterlife. The tools of the tomb owner's trade were also important: architects and other building professionals would be buried with cubit rods, horizontal and vertical levels, and plumb bobs. This could sometimes be quite impressive: Yuya, a chariotry officer by profession, was buried with his chariot.

The objects shown here represent only a very small fraction of the enormous quantities of grave goods buried with the elite of the New Kingdom. In the next chapter, you will learn more about the vandals, both ancient and modern, who robbed the tombs of their original contents, and destroyed the decoration of their chapels.

Many of the vessels in the tomb of Yuya and Tjuya were "dummy" vessels – solid pieces of limestone with no hollow in which to store oils, unguents, or other offerings, and painted to look as though they were made of valuable stone.

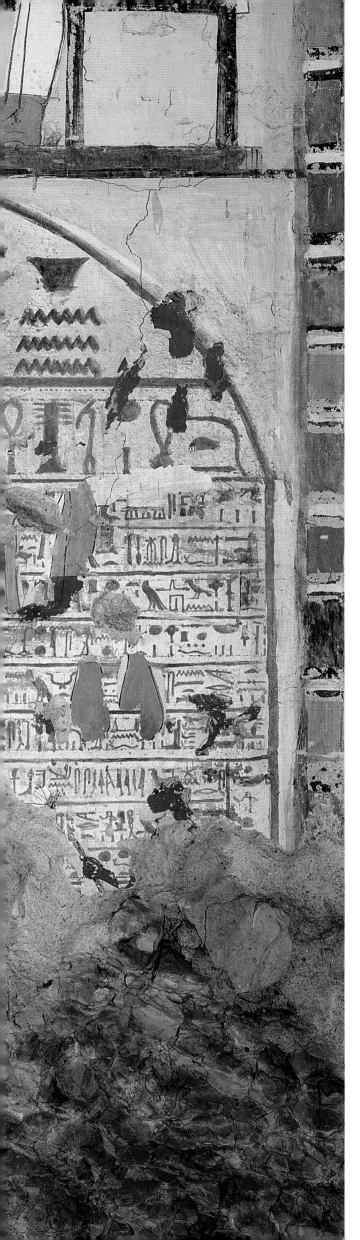

The 18th Dynasty tomb of Amenemhat, Steward of the Vizier (TT 82), provides a very explicit example of reuse: this autobiographical stela, dating to year 28 of Thutmose III, has been painted on top of earlier scenes.

CHAPTER EIGHT

EXPLORERS AND VANDALS, ANCIENT AND MODERN

The original building, decoration, and use of the Theban tombs represents only the first stage of their long histories. Some of the tombs were reused even during the New Kingdom – 18th Dynasty officials re-carved Middle Kingdom sepulchers, and some early New Kingdom chapels were usurped in the Ramesside period. Subsequent inhabitants of the area continued to use the tombs for their own burials, and the first wave of tourists arrived in the Greco-Roman period. After the rediscovery of pharaonic Egypt by the western world, which began in the 18th century, the tombs were subjected to further desecration, and the forces of nature have also caused significant damage to their decoration.

ANCIENT ROBBERS, USURPERS, AND TRAVELERS

After the 20th Dynasty came to an end, and with it the New Kingdom, Egypt entered the decentralized Third Intermediate Period (Dynasties 21–25). Many of the Theban tombs were abandoned by the families of their original owners and were taken over by the new inhabitants of the area, who subjected them to more damage. Secondary shafts were sunk into the floors of the tomb chapels, and in some cases several additional generations of burials were placed inside. This type of reuse continued into the Late Period, and sometimes even the Ptolemaic and Roman eras.

The tomb of the 18th Dynasty Royal Butler Parennefer (TT 188) is an excellent example of this type of reuse: only two of the tomb's six burial shafts are part of its original architecture; the other four were dug later, most probably in the 21st and 22nd Dynasties. Although the tomb was robbed in both ancient and modern times, careful excavation by Canadian archaeologist Susan Redford (see below, p. 269) has revealed traces of the original burials of the tomb owner and his wife, as well as 21st and 22nd Dynasty interments of members of the family of a priest of Montu, and funerary material from the 25th Dynasty and the Ptolemaic period. An additional chamber was cut into the front wall of the tomb, apparently in Roman times. Many of the Theban tombs display similar patterns of usurpation and reuse.

We know that the private tombs at Thebes, like the royal tombs in the Valley of the Kings, were attractive targets for ancient thieves and vandals. The robbers would have been searching for precious metals and woods, as well as the easily portable (and highly valuable) oils and unguents stored in the burial chambers. As long as the cult was still being carried out by family members or paid priests, the burial was provided with some protection, but when it fell into abeyance, the tomb and its contents would have been easy prey for the robbers who haunted the Theban hills. Many tombs may have already been stripped of their precious goods before later inhabitants of the area chose them for their own sepulchers. It is clear that the almost-intact tomb of Yuya and Tjuya, for example, was violated soon after the burial chamber was closed – perhaps even by some of those who had helped to carve it into the rock (see above, pp. 237–39).

Much of our information about ancient tomb robbers comes from the royal tombs in the Valley of the Kings, but it is likely that the private tombs, which would have been much less well guarded, were even more at risk. Our sources tell us that protecting the tombs from determined thieves was a problem faced by the necropolis guards almost as soon as the burials were made. In fact the royal official Ineni (TT 81) brags in one inscription in his own burial that he created the tomb of the king, "… none seeing and none hearing …" – clear evidence that hiding the royal burials was an important goal. We know, however, that the tomb of Thutmose IV was broken into soon after his burial, and Tutankhamun's tomb was robbed at least twice within 10 or 15 years of his death.

A number of papyri that provide fascinating information about ancient tomb robbers have survived. My favorite, which dates from the late 20th Dynasty, tells the story of robberies that had taken place on the West Bank at Thebes, in both private and royal tombs. News of these robberies reached the ears of Paser, the mayor of the East Bank. A commission was sent to investigate, and reported that only one tomb, of the 17th Dynasty king Sobekemsaf, had been violated. However, it seems that the commission was corrupted by the mayor of the West Bank, Pawero, whose duty it was to guard the area, but who appears instead to have been involved in robbing the tombs.

Evidence of later reuse in the form of Roman pottery, shabtis, and human bones (not visible) litter the floor of the badly damaged burial chamber of Amenemhat (TT 82). Much of the rubble seen here consists of chunks of limestone and plaster that have fallen from the walls.

Certain elite tombs at Thebes were also subjected to a sort of *damnatio memoriae* (the removal of traces of a person's existence) soon after their completion, with the owner's name or face deliberately erased wherever it occurred. This generally happened when the tomb owner or his family fell out of favor, perhaps with a change in administration. Amarna period tombs were especially prone to this sort of treatment, due to the attempts by later monarchs to remove all memory of the heretic king, Akhenaten, and his supporters.

Some tombs bear the traces of the tourist trade that flourished in the Theban area even as early as the Greco-Roman era. A number of Classical authors mention the tombs that these ancient tourists (many apparently businessmen) could explore, and many of the travelers left behind graffiti (recorded particularly in the Valley of the Kings) – mostly in Latin, Greek, or Coptic, but also in several other Mediterranean languages. During the Coptic era (from the 4th century AD), a number of the Theban tombs were used as monks' cells, and many of what were regarded as "pagan" images were damaged by the Christian inhabitants.

MODERN SCHOLARS, VANDALS, AND THIEVES

The Theban region was closed to western travelers after the Arab conquest of Egypt in AD 641, and it was not until the 18th century that Europeans began to visit southern Egypt again. One of the first was Claude Sicard, a Jesuit priest who came to Egypt in 1707 and spent a considerable amount of time exploring and recording ancient monuments before his death in 1726. Among his achievements were the correct identification of the modern town of Luxor as ancient Thebes and a map on which he showed the approximate location of many temples, tombs, and pyramids. Several other European travelers followed in Sicard's footsteps.

Napoleon's military expedition to Egypt of 1798 to 1801 was accompanied by a 130-member scientific team who set out to document as much of Egypt's past and present as they could. Their work resulted in the publication of the monumental *Description de l'Egypte*, which included scenes and texts from some of the Theban tombs. The publication of this massive series of volumes stimulated western interest in ancient Egypt, and museums and collectors around the world immediately began to clamor for artifacts, paintings, and reliefs from both the royal and elite tombs. As a result, many beautiful reliefs were hacked from the walls of the Theban tombs and sold into European collections, and much of what remained of their original contents was also removed to foreign museums.

European diplomats were some of the most egregious offenders in the black-market trade. The French and British consuls, Bernardino Drovetti and Henry Salt, competed fiercely for antiquities, employing a number of agents to carry out their dirty work for them. Both sides were known to resort to physical violence, and the scramble for the best objects resulted in a veil of secrecy that has obscured the provenance of many of their acquisitions.

One of the most successful, and colorful, of these agents, was Giovanni Battista Belzoni, who, in addition to exploits such as the removal to England of both a colossal statue from the Ramesseum (the memorial temple of Ramesses II) and the calcite sarcophagus of Seti I from his tomb in the Valley of the Kings, looted a number of the elite tombs at Thebes. Belzoni began life as a strongman in an Italian circus, and also studied engineering. He came to Egypt to try to sell a new device for use in irrigation systems to the Pasha, Muhammad Ali, but soon found that he could use his engineering skills successfully in the lucrative antiquities trade, working primarily for Salt. Another of Salt's agents was a young Greek man named Giovanni ("Yanni") d'Athanasi.

The fate of the tomb of Nebamun illustrates the depredations carried out during this era. Most likely discovered by d'Athanasi in about 1820, this tomb was built for a Scribe and Grain-accountant in the Granary of Divine Offerings of

Giovanni Battista Belzoni was one of the most successful adventurers in early 19th-century Egypt, acquiring antiquities and selling them to collectors and museums. In this engraving, commissioned by his wife after his death, Belzoni is shown with several of his major finds, many from Thebes, including the colossal head of a statue of Ramesses II from the pharaoh's memorial temple, the Ramesseum, now in the British Museum in London.

ABOVE
These lively paintings from the Ramesside tomb of the sculptor Ipuy (TT 217) are badly scratched and chipped, and have been restored in places with modern plaster to stabilize them. In the upper register are scenes of manufacture, including sculptors at work, while the lower register depicts men fishing.

OPPOSITE
Extensive damage by vandals and natural weathering is visible on the painted frescoes that cover the walls and ceiling of the tomb of the 18th Dynasty army commander, Amenemhab (TT 85).

Amun during the mid-18th Dynasty, in the area of Dra Abu el-Naga. A number of sections of the wall paintings were removed from the walls of the tomb and purchased by various collectors. Ten of these pieces were sold to the British Museum by Henry Salt; an eleventh came to the Museum in 1833 via two church ministers, George Waddington and Barnard Hanbury, who had acquired it on a visit to Egypt in 1821. Other fragments from this tomb are today in the Musée Calvet in Avignon, the Musée des Beaux-Arts, Lyon, and the Egyptian Museum in Berlin. The location of the tomb itself has been lost, however, despite the best efforts of several Egyptologists to find it again.

A strong antiquities service was founded in 1858 by Said Pasha, with Auguste Mariette, a French Egyptologist who had originally come to Egypt to purchase Coptic manuscripts for the Louvre, as its first head. New laws were passed, and all excavations in Egypt were, at least in theory, carried out with the permission of the Egyptian government. Unfortunately, many people who had grown rich through the black market continued to carry out illegal excavations, and priceless antiquities continued to be smuggled out of the country.

Some of the native families who lived on the West Bank became professionals in dealing with stolen antiquities. Of these, the most famous were the Abdel Rassouls. Long-time inhabitants of the village of Qurna, they were experienced explorers who had passed down their extensive knowledge of the Theban hills from father to son. Their most famous discovery was TT 320, the first Royal Mummy Cache.

This story has been told many times, but I heard it from the lips of one of the last surviving members of the family, Sheikh Ali Abdel Rassoul, proprietor of the El-Marsam Hotel on the West Bank until his death. I met Sheikh Ali when I was a young inspector, working with the University of Pennsylvania expedition to

Malkata, the site of a palace of Amenhotep III. Each day after work, we would go to the hotel to relax and drink tea. Sheikh Ali recognized how serious and committed I was to archaeology, and liked to come over so he could sit and talk with me.

According to Sheikh Ali, one of the Abdel Rassoul brothers was herding his goats in the hills at Deir el-Bahari sometime around 1870 when an animal ran away from the herd and fell into a deep chasm. The shepherd followed the sound of his lost charge's bleating, and found himself at the bottom of a shaft, with a tunnel on one side leading into a series of corridors and chambers packed with ancient coffins and other artifacts – including the mummies of many of the great pharaohs of the New Kingdom. The Abdel Rassouls kept the great find quiet for around ten years, entering the tomb only infrequently and removing minor artifacts to sell on the black market. However, the royal names on these artifacts soon alerted the authorities, and agents of the antiquities department (including Ahmed Kamal Pasha, the first great Egyptian Egyptologist) traced the objects to the Abdel Rassouls. At least one of the brothers was imprisoned, and probably tortured, and eventually the family revealed the location of the tomb to the government officials.

On 6 July 1881, archaeologists entered the hidden tomb, and found more than 30 coffins containing the bodies of some of the most illustrious of the New Kingdom pharaohs, including Seqenenre Taa II, his son Ahmose and his grandson Amenhotep I, Thutmose II and Thutmose III, Seti I, Ramesses II, and Ramesses III. One of the bodies was originally identified as Thutmose I but has long been suspected by Egyptologists to be non-royal; our recent CT-scan of this mummy has proven that it cannot be the king. Also present were the burials of members of the family of the 21st Dynasty High Priests of Amun who had helped to clear the royal tombs in the Valley of the Kings and conceal the bodies of the ancient kings. It took the Antiquities Service only two days to clear the tomb, and on 15 July a steamer transported the mummies and their accouterments to Cairo. The local villagers lined the banks of the river to say farewell to their ancestors, keening and tearing their clothes in timeless gestures of mourning. The arrival of the mummies in Cairo was less dramatic; because the customs register had no category for mummies, they were recorded as salted fish!

THE DAWN OF EGYPTOLOGY

Perhaps the only positive outcome of the surge of interest in antiquities during the 19th century was an accompanying increase in documentation. A number of early scholars and explorers copied scenes and texts from the ancient monuments, and in

Part of an offering scene and the textile decoration of the ceiling still cling to the rough surface of the tomb chapel of Paser (TT 367), while large areas have now disappeared, revealing the rock beneath. This also demonstrates the difficult conditions faced by the artists in creating these masterpieces.

some cases this has helped preserve information that would otherwise have been lost due to later damage or destruction.

Following on from Napoleon's Egyptian campaign, another important expedition arrived in Egypt in 1828, sponsored jointly by the French and Tuscan governments. This was led by Jean-François Champollion, who had cracked the hieroglyphic code six years earlier, and Ippolito Rosellini, a young professor at the University of Pisa. Several artists accompanied the expedition, and although much of their attention was focused on the royal tombs in the Valley of the Kings, the publications from this expedition – Rosellini's *Monumenti dell'Egitto e della Nubia* and Champollion's *Monuments de l'Egypte et de la Nubie* – include many copies of Theban tomb scenes. The expedition also returned home with numerous antiquities, including wall decoration cut from the tomb of Seti I.

In 1842 a major documentation expedition was sent to Egypt by the King of Prussia, led by Egyptologist Karl Richard Lepsius (who had studied with Rosellini). The team arrived in Thebes in 1844, and although they were primarily focused on architecture, they did also copy some of the scenes in the Theban tombs. Although the exact styles of the ancient artists were not captured by these copyists, many of the details were recorded faithfully, providing important information for later scholars. The results of this expedition were published in the multi-volume *Denkmäler aus Ägypten und Äthiopien.*

Individual European explorers who came to Thebes during the 19th century to visit the tombs included Charles Irby, James Mangles, Frédéric Cailliaud, and William Bankes; some even used the chapels as temporary residences during their stay. Many of these men limited themselves to copying the scenes, but others

Remnants of a wall painting in the tomb of Ineni (TT 81) – surviving decoration in the Theban tombs that has not been removed or damaged in the past by robbers and vandals is now in danger of further deterioration, making the work of conservation and restoration imperative.

actually removed paintings from the walls to sell them to private collectors and museums, destroying a great deal in the process.

One of the first scholars to pay particular attention to the Theban tombs was John Gardner Wilkinson, who based much of his understanding of the pharaonic era, which he published in *Manners and Customs of the Ancient Egyptians* (1837–41), on the scenes in private tombs. He arrived in Egypt in 1821 and stayed for 12 years, traveling, exploring, and documenting many of the ancient monuments. His copies of tomb scenes, while not exact facsimiles, record many important details accurately. During his sojourn at Thebes, he lived in TT 83, the tomb chapel of Ametju (Ahmose). Emile Prisse d'Avennes came to Egypt as a consultant for Muhammad Ali on military matters, but he also made wonderful copies of the Theban tombs. He left Thebes in 1843, and by the time he returned to Egypt in 1859, some of the scenes and texts he had copied were already gone.

Many artists came to Egypt, including David Roberts, who visited Egypt in 1838 and produced a series of watercolor images of the ancient monuments that are still considered masterpieces today. Popular books such as Amelia Edwards's *A Thousand Miles Up the Nile* (published in 1891), helped to fuel the interest that ancient Egypt generated in the imagination of the western world.

When, as mentioned above, Said Pasha selected French Egyptologist Auguste Mariette to head the Egyptian Antiquities Service in 1858 a new era began. Under a series of administrators, for the most part French, permits were required for excavations, and there was some control over the hitherto unchecked flow of antiquities out of the country. Over the following decades, a number of remarkable discoveries were made at Thebes, including the cache of New Kingdom royal mummies at Deir el-Bahari described above, and the tombs of Sennedjem and Kha (see Chapter 7), as well as the coffin and fabulous jewels of a queen Ahhotep at Dra Abu el-Naga. The Valley of the Kings also yielded many of its secrets during this era, including several royal tombs, a second cache of New Kingdom royal mummies in the tomb of Amenhotep II (1898), the tombs of Maiherpri and Yuya and Tjuya (see Chapter 7), and, of course the treasure-filled tomb of Tutankhamun (1922).

Epigraphy – the copying of scenes and inscriptions – continued to improve during the late 19th and early 20th centuries, and came to be supplemented (although never supplanted) by the new technique of photography. The Egypt Exploration Fund, under Francis Ll. Griffiths, initiated the practice, still followed today, of recording entire tombs. One of the great early 20th-century epigraphy teams was Norman de Garis Davies and his wife, Nina, whose 40-year career in Egypt included the recording of a number of Theban tombs. The work by the Davies at Thebes was continued into the later 20th century by Torgny Säve-Söderbergh. The Theban tombs were finally given some practical protection in the early 20th century by Arthur Weigall, then Inspector-General of Upper Egypt, who initiated restoration projects and had iron security gates installed on many tombs. Advances in documentary photography were made under one of Weigall's sponsors, Sir Robert Mond, who invented a method for moving the camera smoothly along a single wall. Excavations continued as well: in the Theban massif, the most successful expeditions were led by Bernard Bruyère at Deir el-Medina, who cleared the town site and many of the tombs, and H. E. Winlock, who worked at Deir el-Bahari on behalf of the Metropolitan Museum of Art and made many wonderful finds, including the second tomb of Senenmut.

The Second World War slowed epigraphic and archaeological work at Thebes, and many of the tombs were actually damaged by soldiers passing through the area. The following decades saw comparatively little work in the Valley of the Nobles, although scholars such as Lise Manniche continued to study and learn from their decoration. In recent years, there has been a resurgence of interest in this area, and, as will be discussed in the final chapter, there are many expeditions active there today.

The foothills of the Theban massif on the West Bank of the Nile are covered with modern villages that crowd and threaten to destroy the tombs that lie between and even under the houses.

CHAPTER NINE
SAVING THE VALLEY OF THE NOBLES

I used to visit the Valley of the Nobles, and look at the houses in the villages that lie above the tombs. I knew that the people dug tunnels from these houses to reach the burials below them, and used the tomb chambers to store the artifacts they had stolen. I still find it astonishing to consider how much of modern Egypt is built literally on top of its ancient past, threatening its survival for the future. We can see this clearly all over Egypt. For example, modern Aswan is built above the ancient town. Not long ago, some people began to dig secretly at night under their houses. After about 20 meters, they hit the water table, and some of them drowned. Because of this, they believe that the treasure they seek is guarded by devils, so they slaughter animals to chase the evil spirits away. In Edfu, the ancient temple is surrounded by modern houses, and in Akhmim the modern city lies above the great temples to the god Min. When Arab travelers visited this area in the 9th century AD, they reported that the temple complex here was bigger than that at Karnak. Look at Heliopolis, another important ancient site, which is now a suburb of Cairo: we have recently located a temple here dating from the reign of Ramesses II, and have discovered a number of monuments hidden under modern villas.

The collision between ancient monuments and modern life can be seen clearly at the pyramids at Giza, perhaps Egypt's most famous site. In 1974, I was working at Abu Simbel, far to the south, with no particular interest in pyramids. One morning, I read in the paper that tomb robbers from the village of Nazlet el-Samman, at the foot of the Giza plateau, had broken into the antiquities storerooms at Giza by digging through a cement wall, and had taken more than 10 sealed boxes full of antiquities. Some of these boxes contained objects that I had found in my own excavations at Kom Abu Billo in the Delta. The head of the Antiquities Organization at that time, Dr. Gamal Mokhtar, had appointed General Auda Ahmed Auda to be in charge of security for the antiquities department. When the robbery occurred, Dr. Mokhtar and General Auda realized that a determined and resourceful archaeologist was needed at Giza to establish order and protect the monuments. I received a telex in Abu Simbel, calling me to become an Inspector of Antiquities at Giza.

When I arrived at Giza I began, with my friend Ahmed el-Sawy, to work with the police and try to find the boxes of artifacts. To our surprise, we did find them – the thieves had become nervous when they heard we were on their trail, and had hidden them in a nearby canal. This success changed my career – and my life – completely. I began to bring stability back to the site of Giza. I also began to love pyramids, and several years later, when I went to the University of Pennsylvania for my Ph.D., I wrote my doctoral dissertation was on the cults of the Giza kings. So tomb robbers actually have had a dramatic influence on the path my life as an archaeologist has taken.

At Giza our battle continues. The village of Nazlet el-Samman has expanded so that it encroaches onto the site of the pyramids. The villagers survive because of the tourists who come to see the pyramids, but some of them have no respect for the site itself, and would end up destroying their own livelihoods. Some of the villagers bribe the guards to allow them to enter the tombs, and to let them bring their camels and horses and souvenirs to forbidden places on the plateau, harassing the tourists and creating visual pollution around these great and noble monuments. Ever since I was brought to Giza, I have battled numerous times with some of the men who lead this village (several of whom are now in jail). They have threatened me, tried to burn my car, and thrown trash into my excavations.

In 2006, although with reluctance, we decided to build a wall around the site of Giza to help us in our efforts to stop the theft and destruction. I was criticized for this by many people, including the foreigners who like to ride horses on the site and who were encouraged by the owners of the stables to attack me. I explained to them that I was not preventing anyone from riding, but that it had to be done in an organized way, in designated areas, to protect the site. Once the foreign riders understood this, they supported me.

MODERN ROBBERS IN THE VALLEY OF THE NOBLES

My experiences as the Chief Inspector at Giza prepared me well to deal with the situation in the Valley of the Nobles. Tomb robbers are still active in the Valley, but we are doing our best to combat the vandals and thieves who continue to destroy our priceless past for their own profit. Whenever I see something that might threaten our antiquities, I must do all in my power to prevent it. I say that God can create thousands more people, but no one today can build the pyramids or decorate an ancient tomb. At the same time, however, we must care for the people of Egypt, who will suffer terribly in every way if their ancient heritage, which is a source of both pride and income, is destroyed.

When I became Secretary General of the Supreme Council of Antiquities in 2002, I knew that I needed to do something about the villages on the West Bank at Thebes, which have a long and checkered history. There were inhabitants here at least as early as the 17th century – a town is first mentioned by two Capuchin monks who traveled to Luxor in 1668. Once the area had been discovered by the west, the antiquities trade became a thriving business, and the population boomed. Both legitimate archaeologists and illicit adventurers hired workers from Luxor and the surrounding areas to carry their tools and supplies, and to do the actual digging for them. Some of these native excavators came from the site of Qift; originally trained by the great Egyptologist Flinders Petrie in the late 19th and early 20th centuries, they were, and still are, considered the best archaeological workers in Egypt. The man who first taught me to excavate, Reis Doctoor, was from Qift. He was a wonderful man, who knew how to clear a tomb or clean a statue with great care. He had been taught by leading foreign archaeologists, and I learned a huge amount from him.

Digging for antiquities provided a good living for some of these men and their families – villagers from Luxor and Qift as well as Bedouin from the desert and Nubians from the south – and many of them decided to live on the West Bank, near the excavations. In some cases, foreign travelers and adventurers, who wanted somewhere to stay when they were in Thebes and a place to leave their belongings between seasons, paid for houses there. These early houses here were of mud brick with large courtyards, and many of them incorporated tombs in their architecture. In the 19th century John Gardner Wilkinson, for example, lived in one such house when he was at Thebes (see also p. 259). Henry Salt constructed a villa for his agent Giovanni d'Athanasi; this was the first modern house to be built on the hills, constructed as a small citadel surrounded by courtyards.

The village of el-Qurna, whose history is well documented, encapsulates the history of the area as a whole. Its full name is El-Sheikh Abd el-Qurna, indicating its relationship to one of the sheikhs, or holy men, in the area; the name of both the village and the sheikh is linked to el-Qurn, the pyramidal peak that rises above the Valley of the Kings. The name el-Qurna can be used to refer specifically to the central part of the necropolis, west and north of the Ramesseum, and west of the temple of Seti I; or, more generally, to the entire area between the tombs of el-Tarif to the north and Medinet Habu to the south.

The view from the tombs high in the cliffs of the Theban massif is spectacular. Here, ancient tombs and modern houses, as well as the remains of the Ramesseum (the memorial temple of Ramesses II) lie close together, backed by the fertile fields that stretch east to the river beyond.

In the 18th and 19th centuries, there were no rules controlling who could build, or where, and many of the villagers constructed their houses above tombs so that they could explore them without being detected. As a consequence, many of the monuments that had survived the depredations of the ancient vandals and the early travelers continued to fall victim to modern antiquities thieves, who had easy access to any remaining treasures. These robbers opened the tombs at night, hacked paintings or reliefs off the walls, and closed them again; this still goes on today. Since most of the tombs in the Theban necropolis are closed to the public, and opened only infrequently by the guards, it has not always been easy to discover such thefts. When I was working in Luxor in 1974 with the University of Pennsylvania expedition to Malkata (the palace of Amenhotep III), I went into some of these tombs for the first time and saw the devastation that the vandals had left behind.

Laws were later passed restricting building on the West Bank, but at the same time, more foreigners wanted houses in this desolate but beautiful area of Egypt. They paid the villagers to build cement structures with two or three stories, and without proper sewage disposal, adding significantly to the destruction of the tombs below.

By the late 20th century, the slopes of the Theban massif were covered with modern houses. Some of them are well built, well kept, and attractive, but many are little more than shanties, truly eyesores that pollute the sites. The lack of an adequate sewage system puts all of the remaining decoration in the tombs beneath them at risk.

Canadian archaeologist Susan Redford has been working in TT 188, the Amarna period tomb of the Royal Butler Clean of Hands, Parennefer. This had been explored and recorded by Norman de Garis Davies on behalf of the Metropolitan Museum of Art in the 1920s. When Susan began work, she was shocked to find a tunnel leading directly from the tomb to one of the village houses. The villagers had stolen the mummy of a child and many other objects. Fortunately, we were able to capture the thieves and recover all the objects. In the adjoining Ramesside tomb of Amenemope (TT 374), which also lies in her excavation concession, Redford found at the northeast corner of the open court the abandoned house of a local sheikh. From one room of this house, a robber's shaft leads into tombs TT 188 and TT 374; a door at the back of the house covers a hidden access to TT 374.

Much of modern life on the West Bank creates visual pollution, as the villages hang out their washing and litter the area with their vehicles and furniture (left). This is balanced in some places by modern art, generally associated with the hajj, the Muslim holy pilgrimage to Mecca (center). When the village of el-Qurna was torn down, a number of well-kept and historically important houses were saved, and with most of the modern houses removed, the tombs themselves will be protected, and the site will look more as it did in ancient times (right).

The villagers also use the tombs as stables and storerooms, damaging any surviving decoration and trampling any ancient evidence underfoot. One example of this is the tomb of a female scribe named Irtieru, Chief Attendant of the Divine Adoratrice Nitocris, dating to the 26th Dynasty (TT 390). This tomb was used as a stable for animals by the fourth generation of a notorious family of tomb robbers, the Abdel Rassouls (see Chapter 8). The tomb of Amenemope (TT 374) was also used to keep livestock.

Near the tomb of Rekhmire (TT 100) is a small hotel, beneath which lies a tomb containing a granite sarcophagus. The hotel's proprietor tells his guests that he will show them a secret if they stay with him. Another house at the Asasif is situated over a decorated 19th Dynasty tomb. A tomb at Qurnet Murai (TT 383), built originally for the Viceroy of Kush under Amenhotep III, Merymose, is now known as the tomb of Mohamed el-Rakbawy, who excavated it under cover of darkness. He was caught one night when he went to a nearby cafe to meet with the workers he was hiring for £50 (Egyptian) a night so that he could spend time with his wife and family.

On the East Bank at Luxor, a number of famous antiquities dealers still thrive. These men buy stolen artifacts from the people at el-Qurna and then sell them all over the world. After Law 117 was passed in 1983, all trade in antiquities was stopped, and every collection in the possession of the dealers had to be registered with the antiquities service. But many people still carry out illegal excavations, and remove paintings and reliefs from the tombs. When we discover these pieces on the art market, we do everything we can to get them back. We are pushing now for a new law to be passed by the Egyptian Parliament that will treat anyone caught stealing antiquities as a criminal and sentence them to 25 years in jail.

Let me tell you of some recent cases in which the SCA is fighting to reclaim stolen pieces of our past. In early 2008, our colleagues at the Metropolitan Museum of Art, New York, who have been our staunch allies in this battle, called our attention to a fragment of relief that was coming up for auction at Bonhams in London. It came from the tomb chapel of Mutirdis, a Divine Adoratrice during the 25th Dynasty, in the Asasif (TT 410). Fortunately, we were able to stop the sale of this priceless artifact, and bring the relief back to Egypt. When we sent a team to the tomb itself, they found that a number of additional fragments were missing;

these will be reported to Interpol and the international database Art Loss, and we hope they will be recovered soon.

The second case involves a painting from TT 93, the tomb of Amenhotep II's Chief Steward, Kenamun. Recorded by Davies in the 1920s, this tomb was vandalized sometime after its publication. A fragment of its decoration turned up in the collection of the Museu Egipci, Barcelona. The Clos Foundation, which runs this museum, agreed to return this object, along with two statue fragments from the Late Period. We hope that other museums will follow this example, and return objects that can clearly be shown to have been removed illegally from Egypt.

If we find that a museum or institution is in possession of a stolen artifact, we will immediately stop all scientific cooperation with them until it is returned; I have sent letters to every museum that has dealings with Egypt to explain this policy. It is essential that all reputable organizations and institutions support us in this, to help shut down the black market that continues to destroy our heritage. We receive much assistance in our fight against antiquities theft, but unfortunately there are still some who do not care.

Yet another case concerns TT 15, the early 18th Dynasty tomb of Tetiky, a Mayor of the Southern City, brought to the SCA's attention by Egyptologists Eva Hofmann and Karl-J. Seyfried from Heidelberg University. First published in the 1920s, this tomb was visited in the 1970s and photographs were taken of its decoration. In 2000, the Louvre in Paris bought four fragments of wall painting from this chapel, and a fifth in 2003; it is apparent that they were offered to the museum with falsified provenances. At least one of the scenes now in the Louvre is visible in the photographs from the 1970s, and was clearly stolen after this time. We have asked the Louvre to return these artifacts, and are currently working with a curator there to clarify the situation and bring the paintings back.

Two pieces of decoration from the tomb of sculptors Nebamun and Ipuky (TT 181) are now in the collection of the Basel Antikenmuseum, given to the museum as a gift by an antiquities dealer. We will be writing to the museum to ask for these pieces back; the museum has a good record in this regard, and has just arranged for a collector to return to Egypt a colossal eye of Amenhotep III, stolen from the king's memorial temple on the West Bank.

MOVING EL-QURNA

All of these stories encouraged me to do all I could to move the village of el-Qurna, in order to save the antiquities. But I knew it would not be easy. The villagers of el-Qurna are financially dependent on the tombs in many ways. Some earn their living through illegal activities such as those mentioned above. Others act as guides for tourists, either legitimately, with proper licenses from the Ministry of Tourism, or simply by waylaying tourists who visit the area and charging them for tours. A number of families run small hotels, or serve meals to tourists. They also have "alabaster factories," small shops where they carve and sell calcite (Egyptian alabaster) souvenirs. It is truly unfortunate that the very people who are most dependent on these ancient monuments are the ones who are destroying them, thus threatening their own way of life.

It has long been apparent that the modern villages needed to be moved in order to save the tombs. In the late 1940s, famed Egyptian architect Hassan Fathy was commissioned to design a new village for the then 7,000 inhabitants of el-Qurna. Never completed, this was built about 3 kilometers from the El-Fadia Canal. Fathy studied the lifestyles of the villagers, and constructed beautiful new houses out of local materials that relied on natural ventilation and were perfectly suited to the environment. No two houses were the same; each was tailored for the different needs of the various families. There was an open-air theater, a school, a market, and a mosque. The Qurnawis were supposed to move there, so that the old houses

Many of the modern houses in the Theban foothills are not well built or kept up, adding to their negative visual impact on the site. Lack of proper drainage facilities also leads to damage to any tombs that lie beneath.

could be demolished and the tombs protected. But they refused, because they did not want to move away from the source of their principal income – tourists – and so the new village was never finished. Some of the villagers did move there, but could not settle, and soon moved back to their old homes. The old village continued to grow and the tombs continued to be destroyed.

For the past several decades, the antiquities service has been trying again to tear down the worst of the illegal houses – ones that were knowingly built atop tombs, and new ones that are poorly kept and surrounded by garbage. The homes are constructed on a fragile layer of stone known as the Esna shale, which is being destroyed because of the lack of proper sewage disposal: the water causes the rock to expand and contract, making it crack and crumble. Always we offer the owners new houses away from the site as compensation, even though they had no right to build their current houses. But the police have not been able to enforce the decrees. The villagers leave their children inside, so the police cannot act. One man even wired himself with dynamite and tied himself to the doorjamb, threatening to detonate his explosives if the police tried to remove him from his home.

Naive foreigners are also at fault. Believing that there are no laws in Egypt and that they therefore can do whatever they want, they pay villagers to build illegal houses for them, which they occupy just once a year. One friend of mine gave a Qurnawi 100,000 US dollars to build a house for him at el-Qurna. I told him that if he went through with this I would never speak to him again, and, thank goodness, he took his money back and canceled the contract.

After many years of struggling to work with the villagers of el-Qurna, we devised a new plan. The SCA set aside over £180 million (Egyptian), which we used to build a new village about 2 kilometers to the north, at el-Tarif. The houses are very pleasant – spacious, with hot and cold running water and electricity. We also set aside an area across the road from the Valley of the Nobles for their schools, hospital, post office, and even language schools, as well as for their shops, so that tourists will still be able to buy their souvenirs. For the past six years, we have been talking to the villagers, explaining to them the benefits of moving to these new, modern houses. Thanks to Dr. Samir Farag, the governor of Luxor, and Dr. Ahmed el-Tiab, who is now the director of the El-Azhar University, we were able to convince most of the Qurnawis to move to these new, clean houses.

In 2008, we officially moved many of the Qurnawis to their new homes, and began to demolish all but about 25 of the most historic buildings. We also, of course, left the houses of the few who refused to leave. One family that remained was the one living over TT 374; the head of the household and his brother sell replicas, and wanted to stay near the tombs.

When we cleared away the debris from the houses that had been torn down, we made a number of remarkable discoveries. For example, when we removed one house, which stood in front of the tomb of Menna (TT 69), we found part of a statue of a woman, dated to the 18th Dynasty, that had been used as a pillar in the wall of the building. We also found some new tombs: one dates to the reign of Ramesses II and belongs to a man named Kyky. To the north of Kyky's tomb are three more (one for a priest of Amun, the second for a priest of the goddess Mut, and the third for a priest of Montu); a fourth tomb, which we have not yet opened, lies to the northeast. We will carry out full excavations of these tombs in the coming seasons.

The 25 houses chosen to remain will stand as an important witness to the more modern history of the area. The Ministry of Culture has set aside four of these historic houses for the use of the Qurna Discovery Foundation, launched and spearheaded by Caroline Simpson. Ms. Simpson is one of the leading activists concerned with the history and preservation of this village, and has collected much important documentation on its past, with plans, photos, and stories. Qurna Discovery will use these four houses as a museum to display the history of the site; this is also a way of saving these particular houses, which have very interesting pasts. The foundation has already restored two of them, one called Zayia and the other Bab Hagar.

We have been subjected to a lot of criticism for moving the village of el-Qurna. Strangest of these was a negative report from UNESCO, based on an incomplete understanding of the facts. In reality, the relocation has been overwhelmingly positive for the villagers. For instance, I received a letter from a man who had lived in the village all his life; in it, he thanked me and Dr. Samir Farag for the relocation, saying that he had taken his first hot shower ever as a result of the move. To those who continue to attack the relocation of the Qurnawis, I invite you to come and look at the new houses we have built, and see how well the families have settled here. And I repeat, families who were not willing to go have been permitted to stay in their old houses, unless we know for certain that a tomb is in danger. If a tomb is in danger, we are not using force, but instead are trying diplomacy. For example, there are two tombs, TT 136 (the 19th Dynasty tomb of a royal scribe) and TT 137, the tomb of Mose (Chief of the Workmen of the Lord of the Two Lands in All the Monuments of the God Amun) in which families are still living. We are working with the Supreme Council of Luxor to convince these people to leave their homes because the tombs are being damaged, and the families have no right to be in them. Recently, Francesco Bandarin, the head of the UNESCO World Heritage Center, came to Egypt and saw the situation. He was happy that we had saved the tombs and taken care of the villagers.

RECENT WORK IN THE THEBAN TOMBS

My experiences at Giza, and my concern for our ancient heritage, have also led me to appreciate and encourage scholars who are recording what remains of the Tombs of the Nobles. We are fortunate in a having number of excellent missions working in the Theban area; these archaeologists and epigraphers are helping us to preserve and document these tombs, continuing the work of early 20th-century Egyptologists. The missions are copying and publishing important scenes and texts, making this valuable information available to the Egyptological community, and are also carrying out careful clearance work, which can often help to reconstruct the history of a particular monument and add to our understanding of the necropolis as a whole. I will mention a few of these projects here.

THE PARENNEFER PROJECT

A team from Penn State University led by Susan Redford has been re-excavating three Theban tombs (mentioned above) and in the process has found two previously unregistered tombs, one dating to the Ramesside era and the other to the 26th Dynasty. In fact, there may be as many as five new tombs here. Redford's work has been particularly interesting in terms of tracing patterns of the use and reuse of these monuments.

THE CAMBRIDGE THEBAN TOMBS PROJECT

In the 1990s, Nigel Strudwick carried out epigraphic and conservation work in the 18th Dynasty tomb of Senneferi (TT 99), Overseer of the Seal-bearers and Overseer of the Gold-land of Amun during the reign of Thutmose III. The tomb chapel had been occupied by local inhabitants until the early 20th century, and the decoration is badly damaged. In addition to copying the remaining scenes, Strudwick and his team cleared the burial shafts, some of which were original and some later additions. Most of the material they found dated to the Late and Third Intermediate Periods, but they did also discover a painted limestone statue of Senneferi's son-in-law, Amenhotep (who was buried in Tomb C.3). Most of the statue was found in one shaft, and the head was discovered in another.

THE UNIVERSITY OF BRUSSELS

Since 1999 a Belgian project under the direction of Laurent Bavay has been working in the area close to TT 99, where they have been carrying out a mission to conserve, document, and publish the tombs of Sennefer (TT 96) and his cousin Amenemopet Pairy (TT 29). Early in the course of their clearance work, they rediscovered the tomb of Senneferi's son-in-law and deputy, Amenhotep (see above), which had been documented in 1880 by Karl Piehl and labeled C.3. The tomb had later become lost to view, and no one had entered it for many decades. In 2006, while working immediately south of TT 29, the Belgian mission stumbled across the northern corner of the façade of C.3; excavation of this newly rediscovered tomb was initiated in January 2009. The paintings have now disappeared from the walls, although the ceiling decoration is evidently very well preserved.

DJEHUTY PROJECT

A Spanish-Egyptian team, led by archaeologist José Galán, has been working in three tombs at Dra Abu el-Naga since 2001. The first, TT 12, was built in the early 18th Dynasty for Hory, an Overseer of the Royal Granary of the Royal Wife and

Spanish archaeologist José Galán is leading a team excavating three tombs at Dra Abu el-Naga, including TT 11. In 2008 in the courtyard of this New Kingdom tomb, inside a rock recess, the archaeologists found a well-preserved Middle Kingdom coffin belonging to a man named Iqer (below right).

Royal Mother Ahhotep; Hory may have been a member of the royal family. The second tomb, TT 11, belonged to Djehuty, who was Overseer of Works for Queen Hatshepsut, and thus was most likely the man responsible for directing the artists decorating tombs and temples all over Thebes. Djehuty was also the Overseer of the Treasury. Scenes from these chapels had been published by various earlier scholars, while objects from the tomb of Djehuty are in museums such as the Louvre, the Leiden Museum, and Turin. The third tomb is numbered 399.

Over the course of their work, Galán's team has found a number of interesting artifacts, including a writing board that bears sketches by an apprentice and his master. During the first five seasons, Galán also recovered about 1,147 inscribed architectural components, mainly from Djehuty's tomb, but also from Hory's. These will be used for the conservation and reconstruction of the two tombs.

In their 2007 season, the team discovered a funerary deposit in Djehuty's courtyard; this contained 45 floral bouquets and a great deal of broken pottery, probably from a ceremony related to the Beautiful Feast of the Valley, as well as part of a statue of a seated woman. Also in the courtyard was a coffin of the 12th Dynasty, containing the mummy of an elderly woman. In the same season, the team excavated two shafts in front of 399, which were reused after the New Kingdom. One of the shafts ended in two chambers and at the entrance to one were the bodies of about 16 people, at least half of them children; inside the other were five adults and one baby. In the second shaft were four bodies, with artifacts dating from the early 18th Dynasty. Also found in these shafts were animal mummies, mostly of ibis and falcons.

During the 2008 season, the team excavated the shaft inside Djehuty's tomb (TT 11), and found clear signs that it had been entered in modern times, as there were late 19th-century coins, fragments of porcelain, an iron lock, and other assorted non-ancient objects in the upper layers. Beneath this was rubble filled with sherds of Third Intermediate Period pottery. The inner chamber is still to be excavated, and it is likely that post-New Kingdom burials will be found inside. The team also found a shaft in the transverse hall of tomb 399. A mummy, dating to the end of

Much of a beautifully painted throne base depicting bound enemies of Egypt – a detail of a scene in the tomb of the Second Priest of Amun, Anen (TT 120) – has been destroyed. Following current protocols for on-site restoration, the team of archaeologist and artist Lyla Pinch-Brock has filled in the damaged areas with plaster, and added line drawings of the missing figures.

the New Kingdom or to the Third Intermediate Period had been set up, apparently deliberately, at the mouth of the shaft so that it would be visible from TT 11.

In the courtyard of TT 11 the expedition found the well-preserved painted wooden coffin of a man named Iqer, dating to the 11th Dynasty. It is decorated with inscriptions and scenes, including one showing the deceased offering to Hathor as Mistress of the Sky. The team hopes in future to discover the rest of Iqer's funerary equipment.

THE ANEN PROJECT
The tomb of Anen (TT 120), brother of Queen Tiye and thus a very important historical figure, was for many years in terrible condition and was completely neglected by scholars. In 1994, the concession for this tomb was granted to the Royal Ontario Museum, with Lyla Pinch-Brock as project director. Over the next eight years, epigraphic and clearance work was carried out by Pinch-Brock's team, and in 2002 a grant was awarded through the American Research Center in Egypt (ARCE) – one of our greatest allies in the battle to preserve Egypt's past – to carry out conservation work. This tomb was already known for its "King in Kiosk" scene, featuring Amenhotep III and Tiye, which had been copied by Norman and Nina de Garis Davies in the 1920s. During the current project, a number of new paintings were uncovered, including parts of a banqueting scene and a second painting of the king and queen. The earlier team had boarded up the King in Kiosk scene, but when Pinch-Brock uncovered it, she found that antiquities thieves had hacked out the bottom part of the image, which showed images of the foreign enemies of Egypt. The Canadian team restored the outlines of the missing figures, basing their work on the facsimile copies now in the Metropolitan Museum of Art.

THE THEBAN TOMBS PUBLICATION PROJECT
Egyptologist Peter Piccione, an energetic man who spends part of each year in Thebes, has focused his attention on two 18th Dynasty nobles' tombs at el-Qurna: the tomb of Ahmose (TT 121) and that of Ray (TT 72). Both these men served as high priests of the mortuary cult of Thutmose III, and Ahmose was also Second Prophet of Amun-Re. Ray's tomb is unique, since it takes the form of a royal terrace temple, resembling that of Hatshepsut at Deir el-Bahari. Neither tomb had been properly published, and both are at risk from vandalism and decay caused by natural forces. Since 1990, Piccione's project has worked to photograph and copy by hand the scenes and texts remaining on the walls of the tombs; a study for extensive conservation work was implemented in 1998.

THE MENNA PROJECT
Another important epigraphic and conservation project is currently being carried out by Melinda Hartwig in the tomb of Menna (TT 69), with funding through ARCE. With portable devices that do not harm the tomb or its decoration, the project uses modern archaeometric techniques to measure precisely the chemical and organic composition of the plaster, pigments, and varnishes in the tomb's decoration. This allows the conservators to choose the best strategies for intervention. Another important aspect of the project is the thorough documentation work being carried out by the team's photographer and digital epigrapher, who record every detail of the tomb's decoration. The methodology used in this project is truly state-of-the-art, and should serve as a model for future projects of this type.

SOUTH ASASIF CONSERVATION PROJECT
In the 1920s, Herbert Winlock excavated TT 312, the 26th Dynasty tomb of Nespaqashuty, on behalf of the Metropolitan Museum of Art (MMA) in New York. In 2000, the MMA, supported by a grant from ARCE, began a project to conserve

Members of a conservation and documentation team, directed by Melinda Hartwig, working in the long hall of the chapel of Menna (TT 69). Clockwise from left to right are Kerstin Leterme registering the succession of colors, and Renata Garcia-Moreno and Katy Kobzeff (at the computer) acquiring reflectance spectra of colors, using non-invasive procedures.

this wonderful tomb, which had fallen into disrepair. The project is led by Elena Pischikova, an amazing woman, with enormous dedication to her work. Every year she comes in July and August (the hottest months of the year) with her daughter to undertake this labor of love. One day, I was lecturing at the MMA, and Elena told me that she was out of funds to complete the conservation. Through great good luck, I was due to meet David Koch, who is funding the excavations of my friend Mark Lehner at Giza. I told David about Elena's work, and her dedication; he was impressed, and generously agreed to provide funds to continue the project. Another problem was the fact that the MMA had other priorities and was not able to continue their sponsorship of the project, but SCA regulations require institutional affiliation for all projects carried out in Egypt. I called Elena and told her that the SCA itself would provide the institutional umbrella for her project, due to her excellent work, which is the best on the West Bank.

In July 2008, Elena came to show me wonderful photos of a lost tomb they had located in 2006 under the modern village, which they are now working to conserve. When they began, all they could see was a crack in the bedrock covered by soot and debris from the village dump – the tomb's courtyard and entrance were covered by modern houses.

This tomb (TT 223), the largest in the necropolis, dates to the 25th Dynasty, a time when Nubians from the south ruled Egypt. The owner was a First Entry Priest of Amun named Karakhamun, and the size of his tomb and the beauty of the carving suggest that he may have been a member of the royal family. A number of aspects of this tomb are remarkable. It is the earliest-known tomb to have employed the 21-square grid instead of an 18-square grid for human figures; this new grid became typical of the Late Period. Also, it includes in its decoration subjects that previously had been royal prerogatives, such as the *Books of Day and Night*. In the late Roman period the tomb was used as a faience workshop, and monks lived in it during the Coptic period. In modern times it was used as a house, a stable, and even as a quarry. All of this, together with damage caused by flooding, has left the decoration in a terrible condition. Initially, Elena was concerned that there would be nothing at all left. But when she started to clear the debris, she uncovered pieces of relief, and to date her team has found over 3,000 fragments – a huge jigsaw puzzle that they are just beginning to reassemble.

Elena has also worked on a third tomb, the tomb of Irtieru (TT 390), dating to the early 26th Dynasty. This was completely hidden under the modern village, and a family actually lived inside it, keeping their livestock in the courtyard and pillared hall. The tomb could be accessed only through a house belonging to the Abdel Rassouls, and the head of the family kept a key to the tomb in his pocket. When the houses were removed, we offered Ahmed Abdel Rassoul three houses and four pieces of land if his family would leave the tomb. Strangely, as soon as Abdel Rassoul accepted our offer, he died unexpectedly. After the rest of the family had moved to the new village, our team cleared the tomb and found a painted ceiling.

Elena Pischikova's work focuses on the 25th Dynasty tombs of the South Asasif, such as the tombs of Irtieru (TT 390) (below left) and Karakhamun (TT 223), whose delicate relief portrait is seen here (below right). The quality of the carving in Karakhamun's tomb suggests that he was possibly a member of the royal family.

LEFT AND BELOW
One of the most architecturally spectacular tombs in the Theban necropolis was built for Mentuemhat, the Fourth Priest of Amun in the late 25th and early 26th Dynasties (TT 34), two views of which are seen here. His enormous tomb was badly damaged by explorers in the 19th century, who removed many of the reliefs. Recently it has been the focus of an important project, led by Farouk Gomaa, to record what is left.

Members of Susan Redford's team, working in TT 46, carefully lift the lid of a wooden coffin to examine the mummy still resting inside.

The SCA conservators, who are an essential part of the mission, took eight months to clean this beautiful work of art.

The entrance to the subterranean chambers of Irtieru's tomb were discovered on the north side of the second pillared hall: a rock-cut staircase here led to a room with two shafts leading to two burial chambers cut into the floor. Elena's team found fragments of mummies in both chambers, along with a message, in Arabic, left behind by the thieves who robbed the tomb, saying: "Do not waste your time, you will not find anything."

THE TOMB OF MENTUEMHAT (TT 34)

One of the most important tombs of the Late Period is TT 34, the tomb of Mentuemhat, who was Fourth Priest of Amun in the reign of the 25th Dynasty pharaoh Taharqa and continued in this position into the reign of Psametik I of the 26th Dynasty. Mentuemhat held substantial power in the Theban region, as reflected by his vast, palace-like tomb. Discovered at the end of the 19th century, the tomb was pillaged by explorers, and reliefs from its walls can be found scattered in museums around the world, which is a great shame. Egyptian archaeologist Farouk Gomaa spent several seasons working here, recording the remaining fragments, many of which still lie on the ground. I hope that one day, the person who succeeds me as Secretary General will initiate a project to restore this magnificent tomb.

THE TOMB OF HARWA

Since 1995, Francesco Tiradritti, under the aegis of the Archaeological Museum of Milan, Italy, has been working to clear and preserve the tomb of Harwa (TT 37), a very high-ranking official who lived during the early 25th Dynasty. Eight statues of this prominent man are known, and these, coupled with the size and elaborate nature of his tomb, indicate that he must have held great power, at least in the Theban region, during his 40-year tenure as Great Steward of the Divine Adoratrice (the chief priestess of Amun). However, the walls are badly damaged and covered with bat guano. Tiradritti's team has undertaken an extensive program of cleaning and restoration, and in the process has learnt many things about the life and afterlife of this important man. They have also found some interesting artifacts, including several of Harwa's shabtis, some funerary cones, two glass vases, a large amount of pottery from various periods, parts of a canopic jar, disturbed evidence from later burials, and numerous fragments of the tomb's decoration.

CONCLUSION: THE FIGHT CONTINUES

Ancient Thebes has been a UNESCO World Heritage site since 1979, but for many years this did not translate into effective assistance for the antiquities service in our efforts to preserve and conserve this area. There have been numerous individual projects and missions working here, but it is only recently that, with the support of organizations such as the Getty Institute and ARCE (with funding from USAID), we are beginning to bring these together into one comprehensive master plan. Management plans are being developed for different sites, including the Valley of the Nobles, the Valley of the Queens (under the aegis of the Getty Conservation Institute), and Deir el-Bahari. We have a French expert who will pull all these plans together and prepare a final master plan for the entire West Bank. Our site management will help us to protect the area from both the negative effects of tourism and the rising water table: I can now say that the West Bank of Luxor will be made safe for the future.

Although the crown jewels of the Theban region are its pharaonic monuments, important projects also target later periods. For example, a major conservation and restoration project is currently underway for the mosque of Abu el-Hagag, which is built into part of Luxor Temple. Recent excavations at Karnak Temple are uncovering a great wall built in the Late Period to protect the temple from the Nile floods, as well as Greco-Roman remains, including an extraordinary bath house and the quay of the temple. Our decision to conserve 25 houses at el-Qurna, as well as buildings at Qurnet Murai, underscores our commitment to the entire history of the region.

Tourism remains a major threat to the Theban monuments, but the SCA is limited in our efforts to minimize the damage this causes by the Egyptian national security forces, who have preferred, since the terrorist attacks of the 1990s, to encourage large, organized groups to visit the monuments, because they believe that this will help ensure the safety of the tourists. When these enormous crowds descend on the monuments all at once, it is nearly impossible to manage them. This kind of mass tourism threatens sites all over the world, not just in Egypt.

The amount of conservation needed in the Luxor area is overwhelming, and we can only proceed one project at a time. By setting priorities and encouraging international cooperation, the master plan is a great help, but ultimately it is up to individual project directors to conduct their work to the highest possible standards.

An important new project addresses the issue of high groundwater on the West Bank, while another campaign to develop a proper drainage system is currently being funded by USAID. One of the projects of which I am most proud is the improvement of the site of Karnak. When we began, the site was under siege from modern buildings, many of which had deteriorated beyond repair. There is now an open plaza, so that, as in ancient times, there is a view from the First Pylon across the river to the West Bank. When we removed some of the modern buildings, we found the remains of an ancient harbor dating to the time of King Taharqa of the 25th Dynasty, along with the remains of a town that was once home to the guards and priests associated with the temple. When I first saw the completed plaza, it was at night, and the lights transformed the area into an ancient dreamland. We still plan to plant more trees, to protect the site and to provide shade; set up more benches on which tourists can sit, making the plaza more friendly; and provide cars for disabled visitors. We have also made substantial progress toward protecting Luxor Temple, and are currently excavating the avenue of sphinxes between the two temples. And the American Research Center in Egypt is running a field school here, under the direction of Mark Lehner, to train our young archaeologists in salvage archaeology.

People in general do not like change, not only in ancient sites, but also in their lives. The site management programs we have been following for the past seven years conform to archaeological best practices and I myself have written a number of articles about site management. The tombs at el-Qurna have been saved; at least for now we have stopped the destruction of the monuments. We are also constantly searching the internet to see if we can find any of the stolen reliefs from the Theban tombs on sale, and we are provided with information by our friends and colleagues around the world. We have had many successes, and expect to recover more of our ancient heritage in the future. I warn all those who try to steal or destroy our shared heritage: the new laws mean that we will treat all antiquities smugglers as criminals. With our new site management programs, we feel confident that our monuments will be safe for future generations.

EPILOGUE: THE VALLEY OF THE KINGS

These site management efforts also include a great deal of work in the Valley of the Kings. I am very proud that during my term as Secretary General, I have been able to carry out major conservation here, and have implemented measures to light the area and the tombs themselves, so that they can be visited at night.

I have also seen one of my own dreams come true. In November 2007, the first fully Egyptian expedition to the Valley of the Kings began work, under my direction. We are looking for the missing tombs of Ramesses VIII, Thutmose II, and some of the queens of the 18th Dynasty. I believe that the burial of Nefertiti may be here, moved from Amarna to the area between KV 55 (perhaps the reburial of Akhenaten himself) and a newly discovered 18th Dynasty embalming cache, KV 63. To date, we have found the flood drainage system that runs behind the tomb of Merenptah, a number of previously unrecorded graffiti, decorated New Kingdom pottery, a relief of a queen making offerings, and the name of a hitherto unknown queen. In front of the tomb of Tutankhamun we have found workmen's huts and storage chambers built of stone rubble, all about 3 meters above the bedrock. We will soon be clearing this area, and then we will see what new secrets are hidden beneath the sands!

The interior of the 19th Dynasty tomb of Nefermenu (TT 184), which is being cleared by the Hungarian mission to el-Khokha, led by Zoltán Imre Fábián. This is just one of a number of foreign teams currently working at Thebes to study the tombs of the nobles and conserve them for the future.

CHRONOLOGY

EARLY DYNASTIC PERIOD
1st–2nd Dynasties   *c.* 3050–*c.* 2650 BC

OLD KINGDOM
3rd–8th Dynasties   *c.* 2650–*c.* 2125

FIRST INTERMEDIATE PERIOD
9th–11th Dynasties   *c.* 2125–*c.* 2080

MIDDLE KINGDOM
11th–13th Dynasties   *c.* 2080–*c.* 1630

SECOND INTERMEDIATE PERIOD
14th–17th Dynasties   *c.* 1630–*c.* 1539

NEW KINGDOM
18th–20th Dynasties   *c.* 1539–*c.* 1069

18TH DYNASTY   *c.* 1539–*c.* 1292
   Ahmose *c.* 1539–*c.* 1514
   Amenhotep I *c.* 1514–*c.* 1493
   Thutmose I *c.* 1493–*c.* 1481
   Thutmose II *c.* 1481–*c.* 1479
   Thutmose III *c.* 1479–*c.* 1425
   Hatshepsut *c.* 1473–*c.* 1458
   Amenhotep II *c.* 1426–*c.* 1400
   Thutmose IV *c.* 1400–*c.* 1390
   Amenhotep III *c.* 1390–*c.* 1353
   Amenhotep IV (Akhenaten) *c.* 1353–*c.* 1336
   Smenkhkare *c.* 1335–*c.* 1332
   Tutankhamun *c.* 1332–*c.* 1322
   Ay *c.* 1322–*c.* 1319
   Horemheb *c.* 1319–*c.* 1292

19TH DYNASTY   *c.* 1292–*c.* 1190
   Ramesses I *c.* 1292–*c.* 1290
   Seti I *c.* 1290–*c.* 1279
   Ramesses II *c.* 1279–*c.* 1213
   Merenptah *c.* 1213–*c.* 1204
   Seti II *c.* 1204–*c.* 1198
   Amenmesse *c.* 1202–*c.* 1200
   Siptah *c.* 1198–*c.* 1193
   Twosret *c.* 1198–*c.* 1190

20TH DYNASTY   *c.* 1190–*c.* 1069
   Sethnakhte *c.* 1190–*c.* 1187
   Ramesses III *c.* 1187–*c.* 1156
   Ramesses IV *c.* 1156–*c.* 1150
   Ramesses V *c.* 1150–*c.* 1145
   Ramesses VI *c.* 1145–*c.* 1137
   Ramesses VII *c.* 1137–*c.* 1129
   Ramesses VIII *c.* 1129–*c.* 1126
   Ramesses IX *c.* 1126–*c.* 1108
   Ramesses X *c.* 1108–*c.* 1099
   Ramesses XI *c.* 1099–*c.* 1069

THIRD INTERMEDIATE PERIOD
21st–25th Dynasties   *c.* 1069–657

LATE PERIOD
26th–31st Dynasties   664–332

PTOLEMAIC PERIOD   332–30

Statuette of Khufu,
Old Kingdom, 4th Dynasty

Part of a colossal statue of Akhenaten,
New Kingdom, 18th Dynasty

Upper part of a statue of Ramesses II,
New Kingdom, 19th Dynasty

Plan of Dra Abu el-Naga and the central Theban necropolis (inset), showing the positions of Deir el-Bahari, Asasif, and Sheikh Abd el-Qurna.

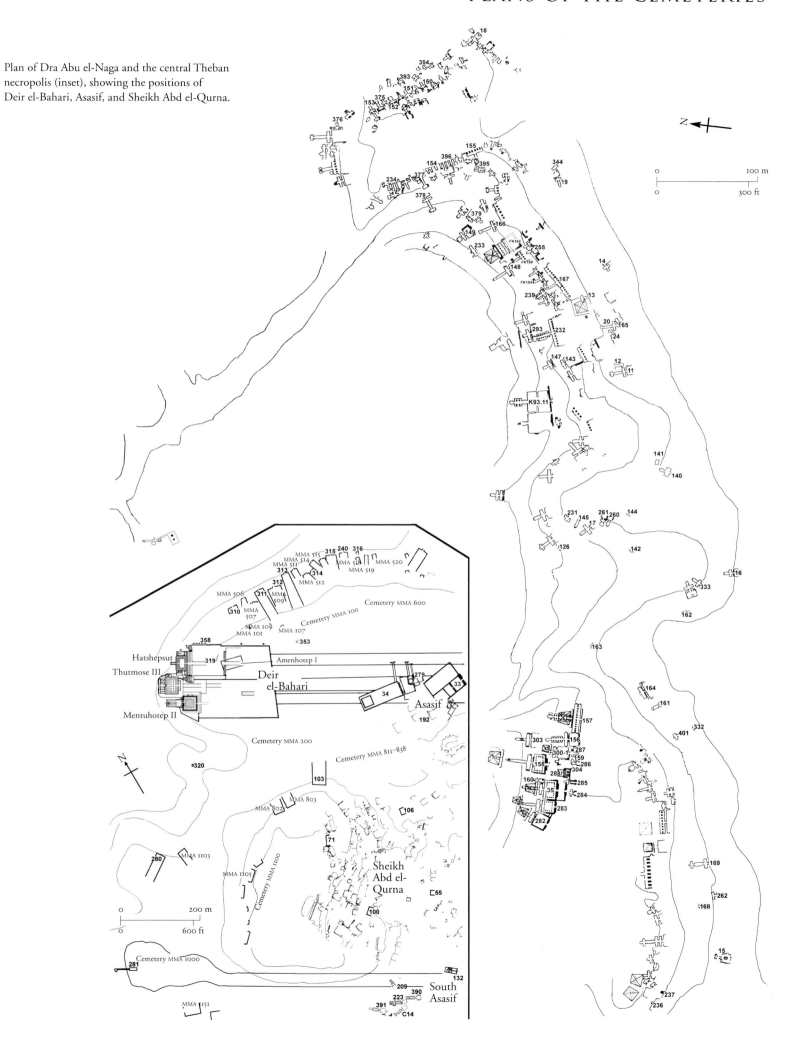

Plan of Asasif and Sheikh abd el-Qurna.

Hatshepsut
(Valley Temple)

Ramesses IV/V

200 m

600 ft

N

Memorial temple of Thutmose III

Memorial
temple of
Siptah

Memorial temple of Amenhotep II

Memorial temple
of Ramesses II

Plan of Deir el-Medina.

Hathor
Temple

50 m

150 ft

N

Village

357

290-1

330

323

321 8A

322   211

10

339

292

321

265

216   6

266

267

217

328 327

340

3

326

338

8

325

356

250

268

329

354

290

335

218-20

359

361

360

210

2

213 9

299

214

LIST OF FEATURED NEW KINGDOM THEBAN TOMBS

TT 1 SENNEDJEM
19th Dynasty
Seti I–Ramesses II
Servant in the Place of Truth
Deir el-Medina

TT 39 PUEMRE
18th Dynasty
Hatshepsut–Thutmose III
Second Priest of Amun
el-Khokha

TT 3 PASHEDU
19th Dynasty
Seti I–Ramesses II
Servant in the Place of Truth
Deir el-Medina

TT 40 AMENHOTEP HUY
18th Dynasty
Tutankhamun
Viceroy of Kush
Qurnet Murai

TT 5 NEFERABET
Ramesside
Servant in the Place of Truth
Deir el-Medina

TT 45 DJEHUTY (usurped by DJEHUTYEMHEB)
18th Dynasty / Ramesside
Amenhotep II / ?
Steward of the High Priest of Amun /
Head of the Makers of Fine Linen of the Estate of Amun
Sheikh Abd el-Qurna

TT 8 KHA
18th Dynasty
Amenhotep II–Amenhotep III
Chief of the Great Place
Deir el-Medina

TT 49 NEFERHOTEP
18th Dynasty
Tutankhamun–Horemheb
Chief Scribe of Amun
el-Khokha

TT 13 SHUROY
Ramesside
Chief of the Brazier-bearers of Amun
Dra Abu el-Naga

TT 50 NEFERHOTEP
18th Dynasty
Horemheb
God's Father of Amun-Re
Sheikh Abd el-Qurna

TT 26 KHNUMEMHEB
19th Dynasty
Ramesses II
Overseer of the Treasury in the Ramesseum
in the Estate of Amun
Asasif

TT 51 USERHAT (NEFERHEBEF)
19th Dynasty
Ramesses I–Seti I
High Priest of the Royal *ka* of Thutmose I
Sheikh Abd el-Qurna

TT 29 AMENEMOPET PAIRY
18th Dynasty
Thutmose III–Amenhotep II
Governor of the Town, Vizier
Sheikh Abd el-Qurna

TT 52 NAKHT
18th Dynasty
Thutmose IV–Amenhotep III
Scribe, Astronomer of Amun
Sheikh Abd el-Qurna

TT 30 KHONSUMES
Ramesside
Scribe of the Treasury in the Estate of Amun-Re
Sheikh Abd el-Qurna

TT 54 HUY (usurped by KENRO)
18th Dynasty / 19th Dynasty
Amenhotep III / Ramesses II
Sculptor of Amun, Priest / Priest
and Head of the Magazine of Khonsu
Sheikh Abd el Qurna

TT 31 KHONSU
19th Dynasty
Ramesses II
First Priest of Thutmose III
Sheikh Abd el-Qurna

TT 55 RAMOSE
18th Dynasty
Amenhotep III–Amenhotep IV
Governor of the Town, Vizier
Sheikh Abd el-Qurna

TT 56 **USERHAT** 18th Dynasty Thutmose III–Thutmose IV Child of the Nursery, Royal Scribe Sheikh Abd el-Qurna	**TT 75** **AMENHOTEP-SI-SE** 18th Dynasty Amenhotep II–Thutmose IV Second Priest of Amun Sheikh Abd el-Qurna
TT 57 **KHAEMHAT MAHU** 18th Dynasty Amenhotep III Royal Scribe, Overseer of the Granaries of Upper and Lower Egypt Sheikh Abd el-Qurna	**TT 78** **HOREMHEB** 18th Dynasty Amenhotep II–Amenhotep III Royal Scribe, Scribe of Recruits Sheikh Abd el-Qurna
TT 61 **USERAMUN (USER)** 18th Dynasty Thutmose I–Thutmose III Governor of the Town, Vizier Sheikh Abd el-Qurna	**TT 79** **MENKHEPER (MENKHEPERRSENEB)** 18th Dynasty Thutmose III–Amenhotep II(?) Overseer of the Granary of the Lord of the Two Lands Sheikh Abd el-Qurna
TT 65 **NEBAMUN (usurped by IMISIBE)** 18th Dynasty / 20th Dynasty Hatshepsut / Ramesses IX Overseer of the Granary / Chief of the Temple Scribes in the Estate of Amun Sheikh Abd el-Qurna	**TT 80** **DJEHUTYNEFER** 18th Dynasty Thutmose III–Amenhotep II Royal Scribe, Overseer of the Treasury Sheikh Abd el-Qurna
TT 66 **HEPU** 18th Dynasty Thutmose IV Governor of the Town, Vizier Sheikh Abd el-Qurna	**TT 81** **INENI** 18th Dynasty Amenhotep I–Thutmose III Royal Architect, Overseer of the Granary of Amun Sheikh Abd el-Qurna
TT 67 **HAPUSENEB** 18th Dynasty Hatshepsut–Thutmose III Vizier, High Priest of Amun, Overseer of All the King's Work, Keeper of the Seal Sheikh Abd el-Qurna	**TT 82** **AMENEMHAT** 18th Dynasty Hatshepsut–Thutmose III Scribe, Counter of the Grain of Amun, Steward of the Vizier Sheikh Abd el-Qurna
TT 69 **MENNA** 18th Dynasty Thutmose IV–Amenhotep III Scribe of the Fields of the Lord of the Two Lands of Upper and Lower Egypt Sheikh Abd el-Qurna	**TT 83** **AMETJU (AHMOSE)** 18th Dynasty Thutmose III Governor of the Town, Vizier Sheikh Abd el-Qurna
TT 71 **SENENMUT** 18th Dynasty Hatshepsut Chief Steward, Steward of Amun Sheikh Abd el-Qurna	**TT 84** **YAMUNEDJEH (partly usurped by MERY)** 18th Dynasty Thutmose III / Amenhotep II First Royal Herald / ? Sheikh Abd el-Qurna
TT 74 **TJANUNY** 18th Dynasty Thutmose III–Thutmose IV Royal Scribe, Commander of Soldiers Sheikh Abd el-Qurna	**TT 85** **AMENEMHAB (MAHU)** 18th Dynasty Thutmose III–Amenhotep II Commander of Soldiers Sheikh Abd el-Qurna

TT 86	MENKHEPERRESENEB	TT 99	SENNEFERI
	18th Dynasty		18th Dynasty
	Thutmose III		Thutmose III
	High Priest of Amun		Overseer of the Seal-bearers,
	Sheikh Abd el-Qurna		Overseer of the Gold-land of Amun
			Sheikh Abd el-Qurna

TT 87	NAKHTMIN	TT 100	REKHMIRE
	18th Dynasty		18th Dynasty
	Thutmose III		Thutmose III–Amenhotep II
	Overseer of the Granary of the Lord of the Two Lands,		Governor of the Town, Vizier
	Overseer of Horses		Sheikh Abd el-Qurna
	Sheikh Abd el-Qurna		

TT 88	PEKHSUKHER TJENENU	TT 106	PASER
	18th Dynasty		19th Dynasty
	Thutmose III–Amenhotep II		Seti I–Ramesses II
	Lieutenant of the King, Standard-Bearer		Governor of the Town, Vizier
	of the Lord of the Two Lands		Sheikh Abd el-Qurna
	Sheikh Abd el-Qurna		

TT 89	AMENMESSE	TT 111	AMENWAHSU
	18th Dynasty		19th Dynasty
	Amenhotep III		Ramesses II
	Steward in the Southern City		Scribe of the God's Writings in the Amun Domain
	Sheikh Abd el-Qurna		Sheikh Abd el-Qurna

TT 90	NEBAMUN	TT 112	MENKHEPERRESENEB
	18th Dynasty		(usurped by ASHEFYTEMWASET)
	Thutmose IV–Amenhotep II		18th Dynasty / Ramesside
	Standard-Bearer of "Beloved of Amun,"		Thutmose III–Amenhotep II / ?
	Captain of Troops of the Police on the West of Thebes		High Priest of Amun / "Great of Majesty"
	Sheikh Abd el-Qurna		Sheikh Abd el-Qurna

TT 91	ANONYMOUS	TT 116	ANONYMOUS
	18th Dynasty		18th Dynasty
	Thutmose IV–Amenhotep III		Amenhotep II–Thutmose IV
	Chief of the Troops, Overseer of Horses		"Hereditary Prince"
	Sheikh Abd el-Qurna		Sheikh Abd el-Qurna

TT 92	SUENMUT	TT 120	ANEN
	18th Dynasty		18th Dynasty
	Thutmose III–Amenhotep II		Amenhotep III
	Royal Butler Clean of Hands		Second Priest of Amun
	Sheikh Abd el-Qurna		Sheikh Abd el-Qurna

TT 93	KENAMUN	TT 125	DUANEHEH
	18th Dynasty		18th Dynasty
	Amenhotep II		Hatshepsut
	Chief Steward of the King		First Royal Herald, Overseer of the Estate of Amun
	Sheikh Abd el-Qurna		Sheikh Abd el-Qurna

TT 96	SENNEFER	TT 131	USERAMUN (USER)
	18th Dynasty		18th Dynasty
	Thutmose III–Amenhotep II		Thutmose I–Thutmose III
	Mayor of the Southern City		Governor of the Town, Vizier
	Sheikh Abd el-Qurna		Sheikh Abd el-Qurna

TT 139 PAIRY
18th Dynasty
Amenhotep III
Priest in Front, First Royal Son in Front of Amun
Sheikh Abd el-Qurna

TT 176 AMENUSERHAT
18th Dynasty
Amenhotep II–Thutmose IV
Servant Clean of Hands
el-Khokha

TT 177 AMENEMOPET
19th Dynasty
Ramesses II
Scribe of Truth in the Ramesseum
in the Estate of Amun
el-Khokha

TT 178 NEFERRENPET (KENRO)
19th Dynasty
Ramesses II
Scribe of the Treasury
in the Estate of Amun-Re
el-Khokha

TT 181 NEBAMUN and IPUKY
18th Dynasty
Amenhotep III–Amenhotep IV
Chief Sculptor of the Lord of the Two Lands
and Sculptor of the Lord of the Two Lands
el-Khokha

TT 192 KHERUEF
18th Dynasty
Amenhotep III–Amenhotep IV
Steward of the Great Royal Wife, Tiye
Asasif

TT 216 NEFERHOTEP
19th Dynasty
Ramesses II–Seti II
Foreman
Deir el-Medina

TT 217 IPUY
19th Dynasty
Ramesses II
Sculptor
Deir el-Medina

TT 218 AMENNAKHT
19th Dynasty
Ramesses II
Servant in the Place of Truth on the West
Deir el-Medina

TT 219 NEBENMA'AT
19th Dynasty
Ramesses II–Merenptah
Servant in the Place of Truth
Deir el-Medina

TT 220 KHAEMTERI
19th Dynasty
Ramesses II–Merenptah
Servant in the Place of Truth
Deir el-Medina

TT 249 NEFERRENPET
18th Dynasty
Amenhotep III
Supplier of Dates/Cakes in the Temple
of Amenhotep
Sheikh Abd el-Qurna

TT 255 ROY
18th–19th Dynasty
Horemheb–Seti I
Steward in the Estates of Horemheb and Amun
Dra Abu el-Naga

TT 263 PIAY
19th Dynasty
Ramesses II
Granary Scribe in the Domain of Amun,
Scribe of Accounts in the Ramesseum
Sheikh Abd el-Qurna

TT 277 AMENEMINET
Ramesside
Priest, Lector, Divine Father
in the Mansion of Amenhotep III
Qurnet Murai

TT 278 AMENEMHAB
20th Dynasty
Herdsman of Amun-Re
Qurnet Murai

TT 290 IRUNEFER
Ramesside
Servant in the Place of Truth on the West
Deir el-Medina

TT 291 NU and NAKHTMIN
18th Dynasty
Post-Amarna to Horemheb
Servant in the Great Place and Servant
in the Place of Truth
Deir el-Medina

ILLUSTRATION CREDITS

All photographs are by Sandro Vannini except for the following:

p. 237 courtesy of Nicholas Reeves; p. 239 from E. Schiaparelli, *Tomba intatta dell'Arhcitetto Cha* (1927); p. 240 (all) courtesy of the Museo delle Antichità Egizie di Torino; p. 253 A. Aglio, *Memorial engraving of Giovanni Belzoni*; p. 262 (right) Petrie Museum, University College London; p. 269 (both) courtesy of José Galán; p. 272 courtesy of Melinda Hartwig; p. 273 (both) courtesy of Elena Pischikova.

Maps: p. 13 Philip Winton; p. 279 A. Dodson, after F. Kampp and others; p. 280 A. Dodson, after F. Kampp, D. Eigner and others; p. 281 A. Dodson, after B. Bruyère and others.

All tomb plans pp. 282–86 after B. Porter & R. L. B. Moss, *Topographical Bibliography of Ancient Egyptian Hieroglyphic Texts, Reliefs, and Paintings, Volume I: The Theban Necropolis, Part I: Private Tombs* (2nd ed., 1994), by kind permission of Dr. Jaromir Malek, Oriental Institute, University of Oxford.

Quotation p. 118 from M. K. Hartwig, *Tomb Painting and Identity in Ancient Thebes, 1419–1372 BCE* (Brepols, 2004), p. 80.

FURTHER READING

Abdul-Qader, M., *The Development of the Funerary Beliefs and Practices Displayed in the Private Tombs of the New Kingdom at Thebes* (Cairo, 1966)

Aldred, C., *Egyptian Art* (London & New York, 1980)

Allam, S., *Everyday Life in Ancient Egypt* (Cairo, 1990)

Badawy, A., *A History of Egyptian Architecture. The Empire (the New Kingdom). From the Eighteenth Dynasty to the End of the Twentieth Dynasty. 1580–1085 B.C.* (Berkeley & Los Angeles, 1968)

Bierbrier, M., *The Tomb Builders of the Pharaohs* (London & New York, 1982)

Darnell, J. C. & Manassa, C., *Tutankhamun's Armies: Battle and Conquest During Ancient Egypt's Late Eighteenth Dynasty* (Hoboken, 2007)

Davies, N. de G., *The Tombs of Menkheperrasonb, Amenmose and Another (Nos. 86, 112, 42, 226)* (London, 1933)

Davies, N. de G., *The Tomb of the Vizier Ramose* (London, 1941)

Davies, N. de G., *The Tomb of Rekh-mi-Re at Thebes* (London, 1943)

Davies, N. de G., *Seven Private Tombs at Gurnah* (London, 1948)

Davies, N. de G. & Gardiner, A. H., *The Tomb of Amenemhet (No. 82)* (London, 1915)

Von Dassow, E. (ed.), *The Egyptian Book of the Dead: The Book of Going Forth by Day: being the Papyrus of Ani* (San Francisco, 1994; Cairo, 1998)

Dodson, A. *After the Pyramids: The Valley of the Kings and Beyond* (London, 2000)

Dodson, A. & Ikram, S., *The Tomb in Ancient Egypt* (London, New York & Cairo, 2008)

Edwards, I. E. S., *Treasures of Tutankhamun* (London & New York, 1976)

Fagan, B. M., *The Rape of the Nile: Tomb Robbers, Tourists, and Archaeologists in Egypt* (Boulder & Oxford, rev. ed., 2004)

Ghalioungui, P. & el-Dawakhly, Z., *Health and Healing in Ancient Egypt* (Cairo, 1965)

Grimal, N., *A History of Ancient Egypt* (Oxford & Cambridge, MA, 1992)

Hart, G., *A Dictionary of Egyptian Gods and Goddesses* (London & Boston, 1986)

Hartwig, M. K., *Tomb Painting and Identity in Ancient Thebes, 1419–1372 BCE* (Brepols, 2004)

Hawass, Z., *The Golden Age of Tutankhamun* (Cairo, 2004)

Hawass, Z., *Tutankhamun and the Golden Age of the Pharaohs* (exhibition catalogue) (Washington, D.C., 2005)

Hawass, Z., *The Royal Tombs of Egypt: The Art of Thebes Revealed* (London & New York, 2006)

Hawass, Z., *Tutankhamun: The Golden King and the Great Pharaohs* (Washington, D.C., 2008)

Hawass, Z., *Tutankhamun: The Treasures of the Tomb* (London, New York & Cairo, 2008)

Hawass, Z., *Silent Images: Women in Pharaonic Egypt*, (New York & London, 2000)

Hornung, E., *Conceptions of God in Ancient Egypt* (Ithaca & London, 1983)

Hornung, E., *The Ancient Egyptian Books of the Afterlife* (Ithaca, 1999)

Ikram, S. & Dodson, A., *The Mummy in Ancient Egypt: Equipping the Dead for Eternity* (London & New York, 1998)

James, T. G. H., *Pharaoh's People: Scenes from Life in Imperial Egypt* (London & Chicago, 1984)

Kampp-Seyfried, F., *Die Thebanische Nekropole zum wandel des Grabgedankens von der XVIII. bis zur XX. Dynastie* (Mainz am Rhein, 1996)

Kemp, B., *Ancient Egypt: Anatomy of a Civilization* (London & New York, 2nd ed., 2006)

Killen, G., *Ancient Egyptian Furniture* I & II (Warminster, 1980 & 1994)

Killen, G., *Egyptian Woodworking and Furniture* (Princes Risborough, 1994)

McDowell, A. G., *Village Life in Ancient Egypt: Laundry Lists and Love Songs* (Oxford & New York, 1999)

Malek, J., *Egyptian Art* (London, 1999)

Manniche, L., *City of the Dead/Tombs of the Nobles at Luxor* (London & Cairo, 1988)

Manniche, L., *Lost Ramessid and Late Period Tombs in the Theban Necropolis* (Copenhagen, 2009)

Manniche, L., *The Wall Decoration of Three Theban Tombs* (Copenhagen, 1988)

Mertz, B., *Temples, Tombs, and Hieroglyphs: A Popular History of Ancient Egypt* (New York, 2nd ed., 2007)

Montet, P., *Everyday Life in Egypt in the Days of Ramesses the Great* (Westport, 1974)

Parkinson, R., *The Painted Tomb Chapel of Nebamun: Masterpieces of Ancient Egyptian Art in the British Museum* (London & Cairo, 2008)

Porter, B. & Moss, R. L. B., *Topographical Bibliography of Ancient Egyptian Hieroglyphic Texts, Reliefs, and Paintings, Volume I: The Theban Necropolis, Part I: Private Tombs* (Oxford, 2nd ed., 1994)

Reeves, N. & Wilkinson, R. H., *The Complete Valley of the Kings* (London & New York, 1996)

Robins, G., *Women in Ancient Egypt* (London & Cambridge, MA, 1993)

Robins, G., *Art of Ancient Egypt* (Cambridge, MA, rev. ed., 2008)

Romer, J. & Romer, E., *The Rape of Tutankhamun* (London, 1993)

Schulz, R. & Seidel, M. (eds.), *Egypt: The World of the Pharaohs* (Cologne, 2004)

Spencer, A. J., *Death in Ancient Egypt* (Harmondsworth & New York, 1982)

Strouhal, E., *Life of the Ancient Egyptians* (Liverpool & Norman, OK, 1997)

Strudwick, N. & Taylor, J. (eds.), *The Theban Necropolis: Past, Present, and Future* (London, 2003)

Taylor, J., *Death and the Afterlife in Ancient Egypt* (London & Chicago, 2001)

Trigger, B. G., Kemp, B. J., O'Connor, D. & Lloyd, A.B., *Ancient Egypt: A Social History* (Cambridge & New York, 1983)

Weeks, K. (ed.). *The Treasures of the Valley of the Kings: Tombs and Temples of the Theban West Bank in Luxor* (Cairo, 2001)

Whale, S. *The Family in the Eighteenth Dynasty of Egypt, a Study of the Representation of the Family in Private Tombs* (Sydney, 1989)

Wilkinson, R. H., *The Complete Gods and Goddesses of Ancient Egypt* (London & New York, 2003)

WEBSITES

http://www.digitalegypt.ucl.ac.uk/thebes/tombs/thebantomblist.html
    A complete list of the tombs and tomb-chapels by Theban tomb number (TT), on the University College London website

http://www.tmpbibliography.com/resources/individual_tombs_number.html
    A bibliography for each tomb by Theban tomb number (TT), on the Theban Mapping Project website